G000256256

ALFRED RUSSEL WALLACE
IN THE AMAZON

Footsteps in the Forest

Sandra Knapp

NATURAL HISTORY MUSEUM, LONDON

DEDICATED TO THE MEMORY OF JOHN THACKRAY
(1948–1999), ARCHIVIST AT THE NATURAL HISTORY
MUSEUM, LONDON, WHOSE PASSION FOR AND
KNOWLEDGE OF THE HISTORY OF NATURAL HISTORY
INSPIRED US ALL.

Wallace in 1848 just before his trip to the Amazon.

Foreword

As someone who has also travelled extensively over the same routes as Alfred Russel Wallace in the Amazon region, reading this book brought back many memories and longings that can only be expressed by the Brazilian word 'saudades'. It is often translated as homesickness, but saudades is much more than that; here, its use indicates that throughout the book the atmosphere of the Amazon region is reflected in a truly realistic way.

Alfred Russel Wallace was one of the unsung heroes of natural history, and the co-author, with Charles Darwin, of the theory of evolution by natural selection. No-one could fail to be fascinated by Wallace's observations on the umbrella bird, or of the various species of monkeys that inhabit the Amazon forest. In addition to evolution, one of Wallace's great contributions to science was in the area of biogeography. We read here of his interest in the barriers to the distribution of organisms by Amazon rivers, which probably eventually stimulated ideas leading to his discovery of what is now called the Wallace line in the Malay Archipelago.

One of the facts that I find most remarkable about Wallace is the way in which he recovered from the shock of the loss of all his Amazon collections, so graphically described here, and went on to even greater things in the Malaysian region. I remember being greatly upset and distressed by the loss of just one backpack of my plant specimens, dumped in the forest by a disenchanted porter. Wallace lost the bulk of his collections except for a few sketches, some of which most appropriately illustrate this book and without which we might never be able to vicariously share his first experiences of the tropics.

PROFESSOR SIR GHILLEAN PRANCE FRS, VMH DIRECTOR, ROYAL BOTANIC GARDENS, KEW, 1988-1999

Preface

The impetus for this book came from a suggestion for a radio programme in 1997. Sandy Raffan of the BBC Radio Science Unit asked me to talk about one of my heroes – a person who had done the sort of work I still do today. I chose Alfred Russel Wallace – as a naturalist he cannot be beaten, and he is a great mentor, even across the years and across disciplines. Wallace is often seen as the 'moon' to Charles Darwin's 'sun' – there is apparently some need to rank the co-describers of the theory of evolution by natural selection. But Wallace was much more than just the person whose essay from Southeast Asia spurred Darwin to publish his theory – he was a brilliant collector and great naturalist in his own right. Even had he not written to Darwin across the seas he would still be a hero of mine.

Many books have been written about Wallace in the Malay Archipelago – the best of which still remains his own, probably the best travel book ever written. He has been the subject of many scientific articles and analyses – and I claim no real expertise on these topics. I just really like and admire the man. I have never been to Southeast Asia and have spent my collecting career in South America – thus my interest in Wallace's time in the New World. These four years are often tacked on as a preface to his major collecting trips in Asia, but they are exciting and interesting in their own right. I wanted to tell that story – unencumbered by what went after – as the story of a young naturalist on his first real voyage.

I have quoted almost entirely from articles and books published by Wallace before he set off on his Malay Archipelago adventure. Many books about him have used the 1889 reprint of his *Narrative of Travels on the Amazon and Rio Negro*, which Wallace also edited, as the source for his Amazonian opinions but this includes some later evolutionary ideas not found in the first (1853) edition. The only exceptions are where I have quoted from his autobiography *My Life* published in 1905. In that book, Wallace quotes from letters he sent from the Amazon – we must assume he is quoting verbatim and not editing as he goes along. Henry Walter Bates, with whom Wallace went to the Amazon in 1848, remained there until 1862, and Bates' travel book *The Naturalist on the River Amazons* was published in 1864. This of course post-dates the 1859 publication of Charles Darwin's *On the Origin of Species*, but from that I have only quoted personal details. Books about Wallace are listed in the back and sources I have quoted from are listed there.

After Wallace's death, much of his library came to the Linnean Society of London. Included therein were his drawings of Amazonian forests, places and indigenous artefacts, each one a fragile postcard-size record of what Wallace saw. His drawings of palms are mounted in a hand-written manuscript later published as *Palm Trees of the Amazon and Their Uses*. The Linnaean Society's careful custodianship of these treasures allows us to see the Amazon through Wallace's eyes, and I am grateful to them for permission to reproduce a selection here.

Throughout the text I have used the place names as Wallace used them rather than changing to those currently in use for towns on the Amazon: thus I have used Pará rather than today's name Belem, Barra rather than Manaus, but have used the current spelling of the Rio Vaupés. Plant and animal names are as Wallace wrote them in the quotations, but are as currently used in the text and captions. Reference on the images to 'natural size' bears no relation to the size at which the images have been reproduced here.

Many people have helped me during the course of writing this book, often providing information at a moment's notice, or reading and commenting on the manuscript: James Mallet; Vanessa Pike; Gina Douglas;

Tony Shelley; Malcolm Penn; Keith Wilmott; Chris Lyal; Peter Hammond; Bob Press; Darrell Seibert; Charlie Jarvis; Ann Datta; Gareth Nelson; Carol Gokce; Lloyd Timberlake; Trudy Brannan. Carl Ferraris kindly and generously identified Wallace's fishes for the first edition; names have been updated using Mônica Toledo-Piza's edition of Wallace's *Peixes do Rio Negro*. Music played by Patrick Russill was an inspiration throughout and Dave Williams was a constant sounding board for things Wallacean.

SANDY KNAPP
LONDON, MARCH 1999, FEBRUARY 2013

A NOTE ON SCIENTIFIC NAMES

Botanists and zoologists classify organisms in a variety of ways, but in this book I have used three categories that are common to both disciplines: families, genera (singular genus) and species, which can be seen as a nested set like a Russian Matrioschka doll.

Families are made up of genera that share derived features which they have all inherited from a common ancestor. In botany family names end in the suffix "-aceae" and in zoology they end in the suffix "-idae". For example, all palms are members of the family Arecaceae, and all piranhas are members of the family Characidae. A genus contains species that share characteristics derived from their common ancestor, and a species has unique characters that distinguish it from all other such groups of organisms. In the early days of taxonomy scientists referred to organisms using long Latin polynomials or phrase names, the first word of which was the genus. Linnaeus, a Swedish medical doctor of the eighteenth century and the father of modern botany, revolutionised the way in which we name plants and animals when he introduced a system of what he called trivial names – single word designations that in combination with the genus could serve as a sort of shorthand for the longer, more complicated phrase names. Today these trivial names are what we refer to as the genus and species names of plants and animals. Our own scientific name is *Homo* (the genus) *sapiens* (the species) of the family Pongidae.

The scientific names of plants and animals are based upon Latin, a seemingly archaic anachronism. One simple reason for this is that Latin was the language of scholarship in the beginning of the scientific age. But there is a more important reason for the use of scientific names. A plant or animal may have many common names, depending on who you are or what language you speak: for example, plants with the scientific name *Hyacinthoides non-scripta* (L.) Chouard ex Rothm. are called bluebells in Britain, but in the United States, the common name bluebell refers to members of the genus *Campanula*, in a completely different family. A scientific name makes an organism universally identifiable, whatever language one speaks. However, mistakes sometimes happen – a species may accidently be given a scientific name that has already been used by someone else. So, taxonomists ensure that the scientific name of a plant or animal is uniquely identifiable by adding the surname of the person who coined the scientific name. For example, Wallace named a species in the palm genus *Euterpe* as new to science and he called it *Euterpe catinga*. When refering to this plant by its scientific name, we call it *Euterpe catinga* Wallace. This differentiates it uniquely from any other '*Euterpe catinga*' – we all know that it is Wallace's palm we mean rather than a *Euterpe catinga* described by someone else.

I have, for reasons of space and clarity, not used authors of scientific names in the captions or text, but an interested reader can find them in Wallace's *Peixes do Rio Negro* for fish and in the *World Checklist of Palms*; both are cited in the section on Reading. The careful keeping track of scientific names makes it possible for taxonomists to pursue their trade, and is the basis for the common language of biology.

Introduction

❖ ❖ ❖ ❖ ❖ ❖ ❖ ❖ ❖ ❖ ❖ ❖

Libraries are magical places. In them are held treasures – of language and of art. Some of the works in the world's libraries are duplicated elsewhere, but others are truly unique, one-off jewels. The Library at the Natural History Museum in London has perhaps more than its fair share of such jewels – but none has been more exciting to me than seeing for the first time the exquisite pencil drawings of fishes made by Alfred Russel Wallace deep in the Amazon basin in the mid-nineteenth century. Any original writings or drawings by such a famous scientist are a thrill to see, but these fishes are even more special – they, like Wallace himself, are survivors of a shipwreck and a disaster at sea.

Alfred Russel Wallace is justly famous for his collecting in the Malay Archipelago – he discovered new species

Letter from Wallace offering his fish drawings to the Department of Zoology at the Natural History Museum. He wrote to George

and giving the Genus, or
the Family of the rest.

Also I should be glad to
know if they are worth making
a Catalogue of, if merely to
show the possible richness of
the fish-fauna of a river in
which so many could be found
without special collecting & by a
non-specialist. They could now
be easily reproduced by photography
& process-plate, and might perhaps
form an interesting little
volume.

Do you know any student
of Fishes to whom they would

Albert Boulenger, who was at that time in charge of the spirit collections. (Letter continued on p.16.)

be useful for this purpose?

They are all in pencil, & were often done under difficulties in canoes &c.

Dr Gunther looked at them some 30 years ago and put a few names, but said they were useless without specimens. Still I don't like to throw them away & should like another opinion.

Believe me
Yours very truly
Alfred R Wallace

(Letter continued from pp.14 and 15.)

of the fabulous birdwing butterflies and the equally magnificent birds of paradise. While recovering from a malarial fever on the island of Ternate, he sent a letter containing a draft essay outlining his theory of organic change to the Englishman Charles Darwin, prompting Darwin to finally publish his theory of evolution by natural selection, which changed biology forever. But Wallace was much, much more than the co-discoverer of natural selection. He was one of the greatest naturalists and collectors ever, and his exploits and discoveries in the Malay Archipelago still inspire today's generation of scientists. He was also the first real biogeographer. His meticulous interest in the distribution of animals, including people, led him to insights about the origins of species and the hows and whys of their existence in time and space.

He is best known for his work in the Malay Archipelago, today's Indonesia and New Guinea. But he did not spring onto the scene as a fully fledged naturalist and collector in Southeast Asia. The tropics were (and still are) difficult to work in – it was hot, the customs of the land were different and in the nineteenth century disease was a constant companion to the traveller. Wallace experienced all these things in the Malay Archipelago with equanimity and remarkable good spirits. It seems as though he stepped straight from middle England to the tropics without faltering, but this is certainly not the case. Like all the best collectors and naturalists, Wallace had practice. His trip to the Amazon – four years of collecting undertaken initially with Henry Walter Bates – taught him many lessons about how to operate as an independent scientist in a foreign land. In a way, his time in the Amazon was his apprenticeship – his master was the forest itself, and by learning its ways and how to find and capture its treasures he became a proficient naturalist and collector. But the trip to the Amazon did more than just teach Wallace how to collect – it cost him a brother, and it almost cost him his life. Returning to England with all his precious collections aboard the trading ship *Helen*, disaster struck. The *Helen* caught fire during the voyage and was beyond saving. All hands, including Wallace, were evacuated to lifeboats and were eventually picked up many days afterwards – nearly out of drinking water and close to death. All Wallace's specimens and diaries were packed in the *Helen*'s hold and were lost.

The potential for loss runs through every scientist's mind as he or she returns from the field with precious collections or data. The time and effort spent is worth so much, but even more valuable are the objects themselves. If one has been to a previously unvisited area these collections will be unique and so precious that a value cannot even be placed upon them.

But not everything perished in the sinking of the *Helen*. As Wallace left the ship he grabbed a tin box from his cabin. In the box were his drawings of fishes from the Rio Negro, of Amazonian forests, and of places and indigenous artefacts. He gave these fish drawings to the Museum many years later. Characteristically, he modestly suggested that they might be of some interest to people in the Zoology Department. The drawings are, of course, interesting to ichthyologists, but they are also beautiful objects in themselves – and to me symbolise the passion and joy of exploration, and, in Wallace's day, its inherent risk. His accurate and minute observation of detail ultimately led Wallace to one of the biggest and most controversial ideas of the nineteenth century – evolution by natural selection – his understanding of this process truly began in the Amazon.

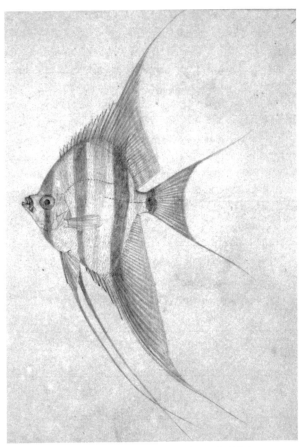

Pterophyllum altum, Cichlidae. Called the butterfly fish by
Wallace, this is one of the popular angelfish of the aquarium trade,
introduced to Europe in the early 1900s.

The Story

"…vast numbers of trees add their tribute of beauty, and the flower-domed forest from its many coloured altars ever send heavenward worshipful incense. Nor is this wild luxuriance unseen or unenlivened. Monkeys are frolicking through festooned bowers, or chasing in revelry over the wood arches. Squirrels scamper in ecstasy from limb to limb, unable to contain themselves for joyousness… Birds of the gaudiest plumage flit through the trees." (EDWARDS, 1847: 29)

What young man, intent on making a living collecting specimens of natural history would not be inspired to travel to the far-off land of Brazil after reading these words of Edwards? Curiosity about the natural world was flowering in the mid-nineteenth century. Baron Alexander von Humboldt had made his epic journey to South America in the first years of the century, and popular books written in glowing and romantic terms about the landscapes, peoples and climates of the tropics were beginning to be written. The American William Edwards' account of his travels in Brazil published in 1847, *A Voyage Up the Amazon*, extolled the virtues of the region for health and commerce, but also described in florid detail the beauties of tropical rainforests – overstated perhaps, but certainly inspirational.

At the age of 21, Alfred Russel Wallace left his family and Wales, where he had been working with his brother William since their father had died the previous year. He decided to try to become a schoolmaster. He applied for and was offered a post on the staff of the Collegiate School in Leicester, where he had responsibility for the evening preparation of the boarders, and taught drawing. He stayed there for about a year – a year that was to alter the course of his life utterly. In Leicester, as in most provincial towns of the day, there was a library – a veritable gold mine for a young man eager to soak up knowledge about the world around him. Wallace borrowed books, and as he had time for several hours reading daily, took good advantage of the resources at his disposal. In Leicester he read for the first time Baron Alexander von Humboldt's English language version of his famous South American journey – *Personal Narrative of Travels to South America* – which Wallace says was "the first book that gave me the desire to visit the tropics." (WALLACE, 1905: 232)

The Leicester library was also where Wallace met the enthusiastic young beetle collector Henry Walter Bates – a meeting that would change both their lives. Up to that time, Wallace's enthusiasm for natural history had been concentrated on the British flora, but Bates introduced him to a whole new world, with thousands of different species, all readily collected in the vicinity and all new to him.

"If I had been asked before how many different kinds of beetles were to be found in any small district near the town, I should probably have guessed fifty or at outside a hundred, and thought that a very liberal allowance. But now I learnt that many hundreds could easily be collected, and that there were probably a thousand different kinds within ten miles of town." (WALLACE, 1905: 237)

The sheer variety and number of beetles astounded Wallace, and they soon became his new love. With boys from his school he went on insect-hunting trips during the holidays and in the library he continued to read and read. Most importantly, he had found a companion in Bates, someone with whom to discuss ideas about natural history and philosophy – a sounding board for the development of his own ideas and opinions. This companionship was crucial to both young men. Without each other at this stage in their lives they might have just continued in their life's trajectory as it was – becoming enthusiastic amateur natural historians in Britain rather than taking the leap into the unknown and becoming men who helped to change the way in which we view our world.

In 1846 Wallace's elder brother William died and Wallace left Leicester and teaching to sort out his brother's affairs. William had been a land surveyor and worked on the opening up of the railways. He had left a small business in Neath, Glamorganshire, and Wallace inherited his tools. At this time the railway boom was reaching its peak, and trained surveyors were greatly in demand. With his new tools, Wallace began to work as a surveyor once again (he had been trained by William as a young boy of 14). All during this time he continued to correspond with Bates, about matters philosophical and biological – he had read the controversial *Vestiges of the Natural History of Creation*, anonymously published in 1844, the geologist Lyell's works and Darwin's *Journal of Researches into the Geology and Natural History of the Various Countries Visited by H.M.S. Beagle*. Wallace lamented his isolation however, and was very lonely for intellectual stimulation close at hand.

"I quite envy you, who have friends near you attached to the same pursuits. I know not a single person in this little town who studies any one branch of natural history, so I am quite alone in this respect." (WALLACE, 1905: 256, LETTER TO H.W. BATES)

In 1847 the railway boom collapsed and Wallace was out of work, fed up with isolation and ready for a change. He had, by dint of sheer hard work and frugality, saved £100 from his work on the railways – to him a tidy sum. His reading of Humboldt's *Personal Narrative of Travels to South America* and of Darwin's account of his travels around South America on the *Beagle*, along with the recently published *A Voyage up the Amazon* by William H. Edwards, inspired him to take a momentous step.

"This [Edwards'] little book was so clearly and brightly written, described so well the beauty and grandeur of tropical vegetation, and gave such a pleasing account of the people, their kindness and hospitality to strangers, and especially of the English and American merchants in Pará, while expenses of living and travelling were both very moderate, that Bates and myself at once agreed this was the very place for us to go to if there was any chance of paying our expenses by the sale of our duplicate collections." (WALLACE, 1905: 264)

"In the autumn of 1847 Mr. A. R. Wallace, who has since acquired wide fame in connection with the Darwinian theory of Natural Selection, proposed to me a joint expedition to the river Amazon, for the purpose of exploring the Natural History of its banks; the plan being to make for ourselves a collection of objects, dispose of the duplicates in London to pay for the expenses, and gather facts, as Mr. Wallace expressed it in one of his letters "towards solving the problem of [the] origin of species", a subject on which we had conversed and corresponded much together." (BATES, 1863: III)

Whether the idea to travel to the Amazon was Wallace's as Bates suggests, or was a joint brainstorm is immaterial. Bates' reply was clearly positive, and the two young men spent the beginnings of 1848 in a whirl of preparations. They met scientists such as Mr. Edward Doubleday who was in charge of butterflies at the British Museum (now the Natural History Museum) in London, Dr. Thomas Horsfield of the India Museum who showed them how to construct field collecting boxes to preserve their fragile specimens in rough and unknown conditions, and the American Edwards himself, who was by coincidence in London. From him they obtained valuable letters of introduction to Americans living in Brazil, who had aided Edwards and would greatly aid Wallace and Bates in their turn. At least as important as their meetings with scientists and travellers, if not more, was their meeting with their future agent; Mr. Samuel Stevens. This relationship was crucial to the success of both men. It was Stevens who arranged for the sale of specimens, presented scientific results obtained by the collectors at the learned societies of London and in general acted as the mouthpiece and two-way conduit from the jungles of the Amazon to the world of European science. Stevens was to remain Wallace's agent for the rest of his (Wallace's) collecting life, and was instrumental in positioning the young naturalist in the world of British natural history.

The relationship was one that was founded on mutual trust and high regard, and Wallace had Stevens to thank for his good earnings over many years in the field.

"He continued to act as my agent during my whole residence abroad, sparing no pains to dispose of my duplicates to best advantage, taking charge of my private collections, insuring each collection as its despatch was advised, keeping me supplied with cash and with such stores as I required, and, above all, writing me fully as to the progress of the sale of each collection, what striking novelties it contained, and giving me general information on the progress of other collectors and on matters of general scientific interest. During the whole period of our business relations, extending over more than fifteen years, I cannot remember that we ever had the least disagreement about any matter whatsoever." (WALLACE, 1905: 266)

Finally, in April of 1848, Alfred Russel Wallace and Henry Walter Bates boarded the small, 192 ton sailing vessel called the *Mischief* as the only paying passengers and began their great adventure.

After a relatively trouble-free passage of twenty-nine days, Wallace and Bates first glimpsed South America and the river Amazon on the morning of the 26th of May, 1848. At its mouth this huge 'inland sea' could only be distinguished from the sea itself by its calmness and coloured water – neither bank could be discerned by the two young travellers.

Both young men were struck with the luxuriant and vigorous vegetation and longed to plunge into the forest and discover its treasures. But first the formalities of arriving in a foreign country had to be taken care of. They spent several days exploring the city of Pará (present day Belem), being introduced to the local English and American residents and trying to find a house from which to set out collecting. Their expectations were high, and although everything had the charm of newness and the excitement that it brings, Wallace could not hide his disappointment.

"My previous wanderings had been confined to England and a short trip to the Continent, so everything here had the charm of novelty. Nevertheless, on the whole I was disappointed. The weather was not so hot, the people were not so peculiar, the vegetation was not so striking, as the glowing picture I had conjured up in my imagination, and had been brooding over during the tedium of a sea-voyage." (WALLACE, 1853B: 2)

"Previous to leaving England I had read many books of travels in hot countries, I had dwelt so much on the enthusiastic descriptions most naturalists give of the surpassing beauty of tropical vegetation, and of the strange forms and brilliant colours of the animal world, that I had wrought myself up to a fever-heat of expectation, and it is

Montrichardia arborescens. This aquatic member of the arum family Araceae is found in fresh or brackish water all over the New World tropics. The seeds float to shore and germinate, perhaps accounting for its wide distribution.

not to be wondered that my first impressions were those of disappointment." (WALLACE, 1905: 269–270)

The brilliant picture invoked by other traveller's descriptions of the land and climate of Brazil was beginning to be tempered by reality. Tropical forests are strange places. Among the most diverse places on earth, they present an almost unbroken greenness that can appear quite monotonous. The wealth is in the detail, and the young naturalists discovered that they had to look carefully to encounter the region's riches: treasures were not going to leap into their nets! The richness and novelty of the tropics are revealed bit by bit and it is the sort of place that becomes more, not less, exciting the longer one stays and tries to get to know its details. In his later account of his journey Wallace could not suppress a complaint about travel writers.

"Thus it is that travellers who crowd into one description all the wonders and novelties which it took them weeks and months to observe, must produce an erroneous impression on the reader, and cause him, when he visits the spot, to experience much disappointment." (WALLACE, 1853B: 5)

Wallace's first impressions of the tropical forest soon gave way to his mounting enthusiasm for the new life he and Bates were leading. The town of Pará itself with its picturesque, strange-looking churches and squares, the Rua dos Mercadores with its shops full of peculiar, miscellaneous assortments of articles for sale, and the brilliantly painted but apparently dilapidated houses were all sources of amazement to the two young men. General impressions of the city were "not favourable", but the men soon realised that the peculiarities of construction were actually the very things which made living in the tropics possible! The large, high ceilinged rooms, with bare floors and many windows, were perfect for life in a hot climate, while "a carpeted, curtained, and cushioned room would be unbearable." (WALLACE, 1853B: 8)

The two travellers were beginning to adapt to the region, and were learning the lessons all good collectors or naturalists learn. By travelling to Brazil as independent collectors, making their way by selling specimens, Wallace

Wallace and Bates were guests at the spacious house of "Mr C" on Ilha Mexicana in the mouth of the Amazon.

and Bates were obliged to fit in with the prevailing customs of the land, however trying that might be. This experience could be, and still can be, quite difficult, but by adapting to local mores and conditions a naturalist could more easily carry out his or her trade. Certainly, the experience Wallace gained in adapting to a different way of life in the Amazon helped him when he went on to the Malay Archipelago.

"… and I began to think that these and other productions of the South American forests are much scarcer than they are represented to be by travellers. But I soon found that these creatures were plentiful enough when I knew where and how to look for them, and that the number of different kinds of all the groups of animals is wonderfully great." (WALLACE, 1905: 270)

Wallace and Bates soon learned the first lessons of any collector – how, when and where to look for the creatures they were seeking. They were on the road to becoming professionals. Kitted out for the field, they soon fell into the rhythm of collecting; up at dawn, spending the first two hours before breakfast looking for birds, then from mid-morning until mid-afternoon it was the province of the insects – as they flew best and were most catchable just before the heat of the day. The two young men dined at four, had tea at seven and spent most evenings preparing their specimens, writing up notes or in general discussion. Collecting is a hard life if one is to be good at it, but both Wallace and Bates seemed to thrive on the rigorous routine.

"We found very few insects, but almost all that we met were new to us. Our greatest treasure was the beautiful clear-winged butterfly, with a bright violet patch on its lower wings, the *Hœtera esmeralda*, which we now saw and caught for the first time. Many other rare insects were also obtained, and the gigantic blue *Morphos* frequently passed us, but their undulating flight baffled

Caranaí do mato, *Lepidocaryum tenue.* "This rare and elegant species grows in the gloomiest depths of the virgin forest of the Upper Rio Negro, generally some distance inland from the rivers, and shaded by the loftiest forest trees."

all our efforts at capturing them." (WALLACE, 1853B: 25)

"We have hitherto found quite enough to do attending almost entirely to Insects only. We are now commencing also at Birds so that it will be quite impossible to find time to make any thing of a general collection of plants." (WALLACE, 1848)

One of their great passions back in Britain had been beetles and that continued to be so in the Amazon – but what a difference in diversity! Both young collectors felt that insects were disappointingly scarce: "We did not find them at all numerous, although of great variety as to species." (BATES, 1863: 62) Current estimates of the beetle fauna of the British Isles are about 4000 species, and in the canopy of a single oak tree some 100 species may reside. In the canopy of a single tree in the Amazon ten times that many, nearly 1000 species, may live, and so the total estimate of the beetle diversity of the Amazon is a matter of some debate, given that the number of species of trees is so much greater than in Britain! Despite the diversity of species and types of beetles, Wallace was in general disappointed with them as a group worthy of study.

"Here the country is very sandy and dry, with, a scrubby, shrubby vegetation; there are however some patches of forest, and in these … many common insects (are) abundant … : Coleoptera I am sorry to find as scarce as ever … I am rather fearful that all N. Brazil is rather poor in Coleoptera." (WALLACE, 1850A: 157)

Butterflies, however, were another story. The Lepidoptera are the birds of the insect world – the day-flying butterflies are often big, showy and brightly coloured, while the night-flying moths are correspondingly sometimes big, but are more subtly decorated. Any traveller to the tropics is amazed by the butterflies. In any open sunny spot they flit to and fro, going from flower to flower in search of nectar and from leaf to leaf in search of a place to put their eggs, settling now and then to bask in the sunshine. Their bright colours and sometimes reflective surfaces make them seem jewel-like against the forest green. Both Wallace and Bates were fascinated by the tropical butterfly world, and both men used the Lepidoptera to great advantage in their later careers – Wallace in discovering and describing species of the magnificent birdwings of Southeast Asia, and Bates in using the phenomenon of mimicry as supporting evidence of Darwin's theory of evolution by natural selection.

"The whole of this valley [the Amazon] lies in the very centre of the tropics, and enjoys a climate in which a high and uniform temperature is combined with a superabundance of moisture. These seem to be the conditions most favourable to the development and increase of Lepidopterous insects, and we accordingly find the valley of the Amazon to be the more productive of the diurnal species than perhaps any other part of the world. Where else in a single locality can 600 spieces of butterflies be obtained? and this can be done with a walk of the city of Pará." (WALLACE, 1854B: 253)

The butterflies however, despite being abundant, were agile fliers and difficult to catch. It must be remembered that commerce was a major consideration driving the two young men's collecting and not solely the pursuit of scientific knowledge. From a commercial point of view the rarer and more difficult to acquire the specimen, the higher the price it fetched back in London. Butterflies were a particularly good bet for sale in London being very pretty and avidly collected by a large community of amateurs with money to spend on acquiring the fruits of Wallace's and Bates' labours.

"Your lot, though a small one, I trust will be found a good one; there are a very considerable number of fresh species, one of which (No. 605) is, I think the *most beautiful thing* I have yet taken; it is very difficult to capture, settling invariably high up in trees, two specimens I climbed up after and waited for; I then adopted a long pole which I left at a tree they frequented, and by means of persevering with it every day for near a month have got a good series …" (WALLACE, 1850B: 494)

The particular specimens comprising No. 605 – from among the one lot of Wallace's Amazonian collections that actually made it back into the hands of Stevens – were identified as *Callithea sapphira*, a beautiful blue and black butterfly. Now known to entomologists as *Asterope sapphira*, this lovely butterfly is confined to the lower

Amazon and is still known from probably less than 1000 specimens. At certain times of the year these iridescent jewels can be quite common, and although they fly quite slowly – fluttering and gliding along – they settle high up in the trees and are difficult to catch. The males are attracted to rotting fish and mammal dung baits – a capture technique now employed by entomologists that Wallace seems not to have used! Females of *Asterope sapphira* have an orange patch on the front wing and look quite different from the males. They are even more difficult to catch as they flutter quickly into dense thickets where a net cannot reach. Stevens, ever mindful of his faraway client's needs, always emphasised the rarity and novelty value of Wallace's collections.

"This beautiful species I find to be the rare *Callithea sapphira*, Hub., of which hitherto only one example appears to have existed in the collections of this country, [referring to No. 606]. ... This is *Callithea Leprieurii*, Feisthamel, also very rare." (STEVENS IN FOOTNOTE TO WALLACE, 1850B: 495)

Wallace and Bates collected together – in the vicinity of Pará and down the Rio Tocantins with Mr. Leavens, to whom they had a letter of introduction from W.H. Edwards – for a little more than a year. They clearly enjoyed each other's company, and were increasingly enjoying the experience of being collectors in a foreign land. They revelled in the beauty of the landscape, the fascination of its inhabitants and in the novelties which every day greeted them.

"The constant hard exercise, pure air, and good living, notwithstanding the intense heat, kept us in the most perfect health, and I have never altogether enjoyed myself so much." (WALLACE, 1853B: 157)

"The Tapajoz here is clearwater with a sandy beach, and the bathing is luxurious; we bathe here in the middle of the day, when dripping with perspiration, and you can have no idea of the excessive luxury of it; the water is so warm that then is the healthiest time. Oranges are about fourpence a bushel here, and are by far the best fruit; large pineapples twopence to fourpence, but we seldom eat them. The more I see of the country, the *more I want to*, and I can see *no end of*, the species of butterflies when the whole country is explored. Remember me to all friends." (WALLACE, 1850A: 157)

At Santarém, Wallace and Bates went their separate ways – they felt they had exhausted the possibilities for collections around the town and in the immediate area, and also probably felt that their commercial possibilities

Assaí de catinga, *Euterpe catinga*. This graceful species is one of the five species of Amazonian palms that are still known by the scientific names Wallace gave them. The other nine he described as new had previously been described by other scientists and so, following the rules of naming, are known by those older names.

Caranaí, *Mauritiella aculeata.*

would be maximised by collecting in different parts of the huge and diverse Amazon basin. In that way anything they each collected would be novel and they would not be competing with each other. Some authors have suggested that "Ostensibly the party broke up because they had collected all they could in the neighbourhood … but, though nothing definite is said in the journals … human relations were not going well. … Decidedly the silence seems a case of Victorian reticence, and whether the difficulties were economic or emotional we can only guess." (WILLIAMS-ELLIS, 1966: 47)

It is important to appreciate that this expedition was not like the scientific expeditions we undertake today – where a group of like-minded people set out to gather knowledge and specimens. In modern fieldwork all costs are paid, either by institutions or by granting agencies, and the entire trip can be focused upon the acquisition of scientific knowledge. Other Victorian collectors, most notably Charles Darwin and Thomas Henry Huxley, did have institutional support – Darwin was the 'gentleman naturalist' aboard the *Beagle*, and Huxley was ship's surgeon on the *Rattlesnake*. Their needs were catered for adequately, if not well, and at least they did not have to make their own way.

Wallace and Bates had no such luxury. The market value of their collections was their passport to further collecting and fieldwork, and they interacted with the complex Victorian collecting culture in a completely different way than did the more privileged Darwin or Huxley. We are in danger of reading too much and too modern an interpretation into their decision to go up separate branches of the great river Amazon if we assume they parted with ill feelings. After all, Wallace and Bates continued to correspond the best of friends throughout their field careers – across amazing distances from the Malay Archipelago to the Amazon basin!

Bates chose to go to the upper reaches of the Amazon along the branch called the Solimões – towards the Andes, while Wallace decided to explore the upper reaches of the Rio Negro – towards Venezuela and the land in which his hero Alexander von Humboldt had collected and explored. While journeying from Pará to Santarém and on to Barra (present day Manaus) they were accompanied by a botanist, Richard Spruce, who like them was collecting commercially, mostly for the Royal Botanic Gardens at Kew.

Wallace's younger brother Herbert (sometimes known as Edward), who was coming to join his elder brother to see if "he had sufficient taste for natural history to become a good collector", travelled from England on the same boat as Spruce. The Wallaces collected together from Santarem to Barra and then for a time around Barra itself – but they too separated, with Alfred going up the Rio Negro and Herbert going back downriver to Serpa. Commercial considerations were clearly driving when, where and with whom the brothers collected. But

Herbert was not cut out for the life of a tropical collector, much to Alfred's disappointment.

"After a year's experience it was now clear that my brother was not fitted to become a good natural history collector, as he took little interest in birds or insects, and without enthusiasm in the pursuit he would not have been likely to succeed. We therefore arranged that he should stay at Barra for a few months of the dry season, make what collections he could, then return to Pará on his way home. I left him what little money I could spare. … I had little doubt that he would get home again without difficulty. But I never saw him again." (WALLACE, 1905: 281)

Unbeknownst to Alfred, who was by that time far up the Rio Negro in unexplored territory, his brother returned to Pará in the midst of a yellow fever epidemic. Yellow fever was equated with bad air (mal aire, from whence the name of another insect-borne scourge of the tropics – the disease malaria), but is really transmitted by the mosquito *Aedes aegypti* – common in wet, low-lying places like Pará. Herbert contracted yellow fever and, like so many of its victims, he died. He was nursed through his final illness by Bates, who had come downriver a few months earlier, and had also contracted the disease, but survived. Alfred, far away up the Rio Negro, did not find out about his brother's death for months. The biting mosquitoes had irritated Herbert; little did he know they would be his downfall.

"By many an Indian cottage,
By many a village green,
Where naked little urchins
Are fishing in the stream,
With sunny days of pleasure,
But, oh, the weary nights,
For here upon the Amazon
The dread mosquito bites –
Inflames the blood with fever,
And murders gentle sleep,
Till, weary agrown and peevish,
We've half a mind to weep!
But still, although they can torture,
We know they cannòt kill –
All breathe to us in whispers
That we are in Brazil."
(POEM BY HERBERT WALLACE QUOTED IN WALLACE,
1905: 278)

Still collecting, Wallace found butterflies an enduring
and lovely fascination and thrilling to capture. Very early
on he realised the importance of recording the places of
capture accurately, and was interested in the distributions
of the species as well as their commercial potential. He
seems to have reared some caterpillars and recorded egg-
laying habits of some of the swallowtails.

His life-long fascination with the swallowtails (the giant birdwings of the Malay Archipelago belong to this family) surely began in the Amazon. In his communication to the Entomological Society back in London, the habits and distributions of the species he encountered are described in great detail. Many other families were also sources of wonder, and he found them to have bearing on his central mission, the investigation of the "problem of [the] origin of species".

"... species of *Callidryas*, which rejoice in the hottest sunshine, and crowd in dense masses of several yards in extent around puddles and on sandy beaches, rising in clouds of yellow and orange on being disturbed. ... In the beautiful family *Heliconidæ*, the glory of South American entomology, the Amazon valley is particularly rich, at least sixty or seventy species being found there, of which a considerable number seem peculiar. ... All these groups (the heliconids) are exceedingly productive in closely allied species and varieties of the most interesting description, and often having a very limited range; and as there is every reason to believe that the banks of the lower Amazon are among the most recently formed parts of South America, we may fairly regard those insects, which are peculiar to that district, as among the youngest of species, the latest in the long series of modifications which the forms of animal life have undergone." (WALLACE, 1854B: 255)

The heliconiine butterflies (Wallace's definition of the

family included the currently recognised subfamilies Heliconiinae and Ithomiinae) are indeed extremely diverse in the Amazon and form the basis for a complex series of mimicry rings – where palatable butterflies mimic unpalatable ones, and unpalatable ones mimic each other. One of these "glories of South American entomology" was named in honour of Wallace long after he returned from the Amazon – *Heliconius wallacei* is part of a mimicry ring containing four or five species, all remarkably similar and all a beautiful bluish-black. Mimicry was first described by Bates, using Amazonian heliconiines as an example – his name is honoured by the term describing the mimicking of unpalatable species by palatable ones, now known as Batesian mimicry. But it was Wallace who developed the idea of warning coloration – the bright colours of noxious species that serve as advertisements of nasty stings or bites, poisonous qualities or just plain bad taste. Linking the two ideas of warning coloration and mimicry has brought about advances in evolutionary theory. Warning coloration and mimicry are thought to protect against predation: would you eat a butterfly if you thought it would taste nasty? Wallace's descriptions of these insects were written before the publication of Charles Darwin's *On the Origin of Species*, but he would use them and their amazing colour patterns later as some of the most convincing evidence that the theory of natural selection was correct in every detail.

"Trees in virgin forest" December 1848.

Even while minutely observing the beauty of the very small, Wallace still found time to see the forest for the trees. After his initial disappointment he marvelled at the grandeur of the tropical forests he went through.

"There is however, one natural feature of this country, the interest and grandeur of which may be fully appreciated in a single walk: it is the 'virgin forest'. Here no one who has any feeling for the magnificent and the sublime can be disappointed; the sombre shade, scarce illumined by a single direct ray even of the tropical sun, the enormous size and height of the trees, most of which rise like huge columns a hundred feet or more without throwing out a single branch, the strange buttresses around the base of some, the spiny or furrowed stems of others, the curious and even extraordinary creepers and climbers which wind around them, hanging in long festoons from branch to branch, sometimes curling and twisting on the ground like great serpents, then mounting to the very tops of the trees, thence throwing down roots and fibres which hang waving in the air, or twisting around each other form ropes and cables of every variety of size and often of the most perfect regularity. These, and many other novel features – the parasitic plants growing on the trunks and branches, the wonderful variety of the foliage, the strange fruits and seeds that lie rotting on the ground – taken altogether surpass description, and produce feelings in the beholder of admiration and awe." (WALLACE, 1905: 270, LETTER TO THE MECHANICS INSTITUTION OF NEATH)

Forest giant sketched near Pará, December 1848.

The gloom and solemnity of the forest interior are striking and amaze all travellers to the tropics – forest interiors have been likened to cathedrals by many. But this grandeur can also be frustrating to a collector interested in obtaining specimens of plants in flower. Rainforest trees bloom high in the canopy, and a collector down below can find getting them difficult. Green is the dominant colour in a tropical rainforest – although there are many shades of it to be sure. In this sea of green, splashes of bright colour are startling and attract the attention of not only the odd, passing human being but more importantly the animals of the forest.

"There is grandeur and solemnity in the tropical forest, but little of beauty or brilliancy of colour. … It is on the roadside and on the river's banks, that we see all the beauty of the tropical vegetation. There we find a mass of bushes and shrubs and trees of every height, rising over one another, all exposed to the bright light and fresh air; and putting forth, within reach, their flowers and fruit, which in the forest, only grow far up on the topmost branches. Bright flowers and green foliage combine their charms, and climbers with their flowery festoons cover over the bare and decaying stems." (WALLACE, 1850B: 440–441)

But Wallace was not really interested in collecting plants and making proper botanical specimens, despite his early start in botany back in England. He was clearly too busy with birds and insects to dedicate himself to plant collection, a time-consuming process which in Wallace's day involved endless changing of blotting papers on pressed plants laid out in the sun to dry. Today's plant collectors have it easy: we dry out plants over heat and can preserve material in alcohol until we get to adequate drying facilities. Wallace's interest in the plants of the Amazon ran more to the "singular forms" found in the tropical forests. If colour is hard to come by, then the eye is drawn to peculiar form and structures. Like Humboldt and Martius before him, Wallace became interested in palms.

"Everywhere too rise the graceful Palms, true denizens of the tropics, of which they are the most striking and characteristic feature. In the districts where I visited they were everywhere abundant, and I soon became interested in them, from their great variety and beauty of form and the many uses to which they are applied." (WALLACE, 1853A: IV)

Palms conjure up images of the tropics to anyone seeing them. Their tall slender trunks and graceful fronds are the epitome of tropical vegetation. Palms fascinated Wallace because they were "almost all useful to man". Today they are of interest for the same reason. In tropical forests they represent shelter, food and sometimes a way of earning a living. Leaves are used as roof thatch and

Leopoldinia piassaba.

are gathered one by one from the plants, and the palm itself is left to produce more leaves for the future – a truly renewable resource! Fruits of palms are important sources of fats, oils and vitamins. But the fruits are not the only parts of the palm to provide food. The tender, new growth leaf buds, known as hearts of palm, are harvested and sold, although in many species the plant must be killed to extract them. In some species the hearts themselves are edible but often the hearts are valued for what they contain – a tropical delicacy – large beetle grubs, the size of a thumb, which feed on the soft tissue. These grubs are much prized by local people and are an important source of fats – they are eaten alive as a trail-side snack or are roasted in the fire; they are quite delicious if one does not think too much about what one is eating.

A decent specimen of a palm is a difficult thing to prepare – it can take an entire day to prepare a proper collection of one of the larger species. Wallace made up for the difficulty in collecting by sketching the living plants in their native habitats – today's equivalent would be taking a good quality photograph. The distributions of the species of palms also intrigued Wallace – many

Piassaba, *Leopoldinia piassaba*. "I have little hesitation in referring [this tree] to the genus *Leopoldinia*, though I have never seen it in flower or in fruit. The texture and form of the leaves, the peculiar branching of the spadix, and the extraordinary development of the fibres from the margins of the sheathing petioles, show it to be very closely allied to the other species of the genus."

species grew only in very localised patches or in specific habitats, and as he travelled he observed closely related species and their distributions very carefully.

"The distribution of this tree [piassaba] is very peculiar. It grows in swampy or partially flooded lands and the banks of the black-water rivers. It is first found on the river Padauarí, a tributary of the Rio Negro on its northern side, about 400 miles above Barra, but whose waters are not so black as the Rio Negro. The Piassaba is found from near the mouth to more than a hundred miles up, where it ceases. On the banks of the Rio Negro itself not a tree is to be seen. The next river, the Darahá, also contains

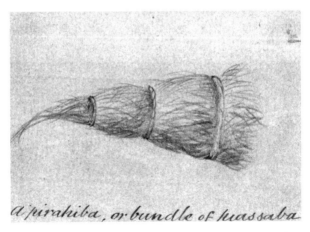

"A pirahiba, or bundle of piassaba." Piassaba fibre is transported in conical bundles about a metre high, which are stored standing on their broad end.

some. The next two, the Marvihá and the Cababurís, are white-water rivers and have no Piassaba. On the S. bank, though all the rivers are black water, there is no Piassaba till we reach the Marié, not far below St. Gabriel. Here it is extensively cut for about a hundred miles up, but there is still none immediately at the mouth or on the banks of the Rio Negro. The next rivers, the Curicuríarí, the great river Uaupés, and the Isánna, though all black-water have none; while further on in the Xié, it again appears. On entering Venezuela it is found near the banks of the Rio Negro, and is abundant all up to its sources, and again the Temí and Atabapó, black-water tributaries of the Orinoco. This seems to be its northern limit, and I cannot hear of its again appearing in any part of the Amazon or Orinoco or their tributaries. It is thus entirely restricted to a district about 300 miles from N. to S. and an equal distance from E. to W. I am enabled to so exactly mark out its range, from having resided more than two years in various parts of the Rio Negro, among people whose principal occupation consisted in obtaining the fibrous covering of this tree, and from whom no locality for it can have remained undiscovered, assisted as they are by the Indians, whose home is the forest, and who are almost as well acquainted with its trackless depths as we are with the well-beaten roads of our own island." (WALLACE, 1853A: 18–20)

Wallace was particularly thrilled to discover the identity of this palm. It was called chíquichíqui by the great explorer Humboldt but in Brazil its common name was, and is, piassaba. Wallace honoured local usage by giving it the scientific name of *Leopoldinia piassaba*. The piassaba palm is one of several species described by Wallace as new to science in his little book *Palm Trees of the Amazon and Their Uses*. The piassaba palm has a peculiar shaggy appearance due to the persistence of the fibrous leaf bases. It is this shaggy covering that was so prized by local people such that Wallace was able to map the exact distribution of the plant. In Wallace's day piassaba fibre was exported from Brazil to England and used in the construction of brooms for street-sweeping, and the fibre has remained an important commercial item today with production measured in tons in the countries where this species grows. The fibre is still packed in the conical bundles like those Wallace saw, and is considered valuable enough for it to warrant air-freighting from the Colombian Amazon to Bogotá, the capital of Colombia, high in the Andes.

"The fibrous or hairy covering of the stem is an extensive article of commerce in the countries in which it grows. It seems to have been used by the Brazilians from a very early period to form cables for the canoes navigating the Amazon. It is well adapted for this purpose, as it is light (the cables made of it not sinking in water) and very durable. It twists readily and firmly into cordage from the fibres being rough-edged, and it is very abundant, and is procured and manufactured by the

Indians, piassaba ropes are much cheaper than any other kind of cordage. … It is cut with knives by men, women and children, from the upper part of the younger trees, so as to secure the freshest fibres, the taller trees which have only the old and half-rotten portion within reach, being left untouched. It is said to grow again in five or six years, the fibres being produced at the bases of the new leaves." (WALLACE, 1853A: 18)

Baccába, *Oenocarpus bacaba*. "A very beautiful oil is sometimes extracted from the [fruit] pulp by pressure; it is perfectly clear, liquid and inodorous; and serves as a substitute for olive oil, as well as being very good for lamps…"

Wallace noticed that unlike other trees, palms often grew in huge monospecific stands – like beech or oak forests of the northern hemisphere with large tracts of land covered with a single species of tree. The mirití palm (*Mauritia flexuosa*) was one such. Wallace also described a new species; *Mauritia carana* (see p.104), which grew not in large stands in flooded or semi-flooded lowlands, but instead in scrubby vegetation out of reach of the highest flood. However, it was the sheer size and grandeur of the mirití that took Wallace's breath away.

"This is the most noble and majestic of the American Palms. It grows to a height of eighty or a hundred feet. The stem is straight and smooth, about five feet in circumference, often perfectly cylindrical, but sometimes swollen near the middle or towards the top so that the bottom is always the thinnest part. The leaves spread out in every direction from the top of the stem. They are very large and fan-shaped, the leaflets spreading out rigidly on all sides and only drooping at the tips and at the midrib or elongation of the petiole. The leaves stand on long stalks which are very straight and thick, and much swollen at the base which clasps the stem. A full-grown fallen leaf of this tree is a grand sight. The expanded sheathing base is a

Mirití, *Mauritia flexuosa*. The leaves are "tied in bundles and dried, and are afterwards twisted by rolling on the breast or thigh into string, or with the fingers into thicker cord. The article most commonly made from it is the 'rede', or netted hammock, which is the universal bed of the native tribes of the Amazon."

Iriartea ventricosa.

foot in diameter; the petiole is a solid beam ten or twelve feet long, and the leaf itself is nine or ten in diameter. An entire leaf is a load for a man. The mirití is a social palm, covering large tracts of tide-flooded lands on the Lower Amazon. In these places there is no underwood to break the view among interminable ranges of huge columnar stems rising undisturbed by branch or leaf to the height of eighty or a hundred feet, – a vast natural temple which does not yield in grandeur or sublimity to those of Palmyra or Athens." (WALLACE, 1853A: 47–50)

The peculiar forms of palms fascinated Wallace and, despite their size and the difficulty with which they were collected, he continued sketching and describing them throughout his travels. He came across palms that had been described by previous travellers and naturalists, such as the piassaba described above or the very peculiar species he found along a small stream up the Rio Vaupés.

"… the singular palm called "Paxiúba barriguda" (the big-bellied paxiúba). It is a fine, tall, rather slender tree, with a head of very elegant curled leaves. At the base of

Pashiúba barriguda, *Iriartea deltoidea*. This species was known to Wallace and Spruce as *Iriartea ventricosa*. It is widely used throughout the Amazon basin for building – a floor made from the stems can last for 25 years or more – and a multitude of other uses. "…the wood of this tree is very hard, heavy and black, and is used by the Indians for making harpoons and spears…The swollen part of the stem is sometimes cut down and made into a canoe, when one is required in a hurry…"

Jupatí, *Raphia taedigera*. "This is one of the most striking of the many noble Palms which grow on the rich alluvium of the Amazon."

the stem is a conical mass of air-roots, five or six feet high, more or less developed in all the species of this genus. But the peculiar character from which it derives its name is, that the stem at rather more than halfway up swells suddenly out to double its former thickness or more, and after a short distance again contracts, and continues cylindrical to the top. It is only by seeing great numbers of these trees, all with this character more or less palpable, that one can believe it is not an accidental circumstance in the individual tree, instead of being truly characteristic of the species. It is the *Iriartea ventricosa* of Martius." (WALLACE, 1853B: 289)

Wallace published his little book on the palm trees of the Amazon in 1853. Mostly it received good reviews, but in the Amazon his friend and previous collecting partner Richard Spruce was somewhat more critical. Spruce was a trained botanist and had earlier, when both men were still in the Amazon, offered to collaborate with Wallace in the production of a book on palms after seeing Wallace's sketches. Wallace turned him down, and as he returned to England before Spruce, Spruce relaxed his own work as he was sure Wallace would publish first. In a letter to Sir William Hooker, the director of the Royal Botanic Gardens at Kew, he gave his opinion of the book, which echoes that of Hooker's earlier, rather negative, review of Wallace's work: "This work is certainly more suited to the drawing room table than to the library of a botanist." (HOOKER, 1854: 62)

"You asked me about Wallace's Palms ... He has sent me a copy – the figures are very pretty, and with some of them he has been very successful. I may instance the figs of *Raphia taedigera* and *Acrocomia sclerocarpa*. The worst figure in the book is that of *Iriartea ventricosa*. The most striking fault of nearly all the figs of the larger species is that the stem is much too thick compared with the length of the fronds, and that the latter has only half as many pinnae as they ought to have. The descriptions are worse than nothing, in many cases not mentioning a single circumstance that a botanist would most desire to know; but the accounts of the uses are good. His *Leopoldinia Piassaba* and *Mauritia Carana* are two magnificent new palms, both correctly referred to their genus; but the former has been figured from a stunted specimen." (SPRUCE, 1855)

Wallace had produced a popular, readable book on palms for a non-botanical public from memory, while the botanists wanted a scientific treatise. The debate as to how to present information on plants and animals goes on today. The popularisation of science and especially of natural history means that field guides, books intended for a general non-specialist audience, are increasingly in demand. If the conservation of biodiversity is to really happen, everyone, from scientists to schoolchildren must care about it and think it worth saving. This can only come about through knowledge – and field guides have a crucial role to play in this regard. Today many groups of organisms are sufficiently well-known so that guides can be written describing them in simple language and illustrations provided so that a user can match his or her observation with a standard, or an example. Many thousands of us go bird-watching, and we do not take the latest monograph on the ducks, we take a small, concise birdbook. Wallace's palm book is that sort of thing: a concise book, with interesting information on the uses of this fascinating group of plants. Hooker was right, it did belong on the drawing room table, bringing botanical knowledge and wonder to everyone, not just the select few. Wallace was working from memory, his sketches, and with limited information from other sources, producing a work that would share his enthusiasm about palms with the general public – about 100 years ahead of his time!

Piratipióca, *Cyphocharax abramoides*, Characidae, Rio Negro.

As Wallace went from the river Amazon, a huge muddy, or white-water river, to the Rio Negro, he could not but help notice the difference in the water. These huge rivers are not necessarily boiling with rapids, the whitewater of rafting enthusiasts; the term in its Amazonian sense refers to sediment content. White-water is really a misnomer – the white-water rivers are the brown, muddy ones, with tons of suspended sediment. It was estimated at the beginning of the twentieth century that a thousand million tons of sediment flowed from the mouth of the Amazon into the Atlantic Ocean every year. If that was the case nearly a hundred years ago, then imagine the tonnage that must be washing into the sea now that deforestation has accelerated to such an alarming extent. The white-water rivers flow from west to east; they originate in the Andes – a relatively young, relatively soft mountain range. The source of the Amazon is in the central Peruvian Andes – mere youngsters at only about 30 to 100 million years old.

The main rivers flowing into the Amazon from the south and north are very different. Those flowing from the south, like the Tapajóz in whose waters Wallace and Bates luxuriously bathed, are generally deep blue-green and very clear. They flow out of hills of ancient crystalline rock – the Brazilian Shield. But it is the rivers flowing from the north, from the Guyana Shield, which are the strangest of all. These rivers also flow through ancient rock; the Guyana Shield dates from the Precambrian – some 2500 million years ago. These rocks formed the crystalline, highly compressed core of the ancient continent of Gondwanaland, and pre-date life itself. The water in these rivers is described as black, but it is really more reddish in colour; bathing in such a river is like taking a dip in a very strong cup of tea. The water is perfectly clear, almost devoid of nutrients, and extremely acidic.

"On the 31st of December, 1849, we arrived at the city of Barra on the Rio Negro. On the evening of the 30th the sun had set on the Amazon, but we continued rowing until late at night, when we reached some rocks at the mouth of the Rio Negro and caught some fine fish in the shallows. In the morning we looked with surprise at the wonderful change in the water around us. We might have fancied ourselves on the river Styx, for it was black as ink in every direction, except where the white sand, seen at the depth of a few feet through its dusky wave, appeared of a golden hue. The water itself is of a pale brown colour, the tinge being just perceptible in a glass, while in deep water it appears jet black, and well deserves its name of Rio Negro – 'black river'." (WALLACE, 1853B: 163–164)

It was along these black-water rivers, north of Barra, that Wallace would spend most of the rest of his stay in the Amazon. The insects along these rivers were distinct from those nearer Pará and Wallace carefully noted differences

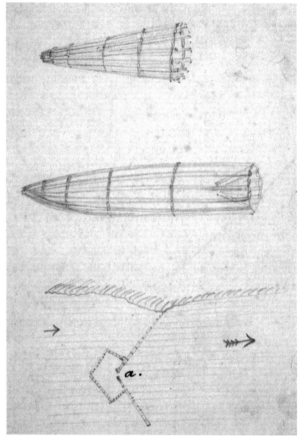

Conical cane fish traps placed with the broad end in the current. The fish swim in, but cannot get out. The bottom sketch is a weir for use with timbó.

in distribution, habitat and habit. With experience he had become not only a very observant collector, but an exceptionally observant one, such that he was recognising novelties as he went into new territory. Along the Rio Negro he began to collect not only the insects and birds so necessary for the commercial collector, but he branched out and became interested in the many species of fish. Since so much of his travelling was done by canoe, this seems a logical step for an naturalist to take, and Wallace characteristically plunged right in and took full advantage of his situation. He found the differences between the fishes of white-water and black-water fascinating, and when the opportunity arose, he not only collected fish, but sketched them as they were pulled from the water. As he went further and further up the Rio Negro and then the Rio Vaupés, he discovered more and more to fascinate him.

"The small fishes of these rivers are in wonderful variety, and the large proportion of species here, different from those I had observed in the Rio Negro, led me to hope that in the upper parts of the river I should find them almost entirely new." (WALLACE, 1853B: 309)

"As might be expected in the greatest river in the world, there is a corresponding abundance and variety of fish. They supply the Indians with the greater part of their animal food, and are at all times more plentiful, and easier to be obtained, than birds or game from the forest." (WALLACE, 1853B: 467)

Wallace's local companions and servants understood catching fish – after all, fish are the staple diet of people living along the Amazon and in the dry season when the rivers are relatively low and the fishes are abundant, whole communities will move to temporary villages along rapids to fish. The catch is then salted and dried, thus preserving it for the rest of the year, when fishes may be harder to come by. The theme of fish as food permeates Wallace's writings from the Amazon – but even hungry, he could not resist observing and recording what he saw.

"On my return to Pimichin I found that my Indians had had but little success in fishing, three or four small

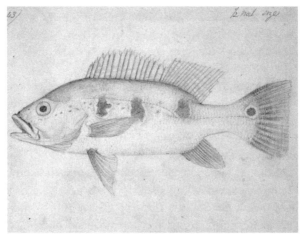

Tucurané atowa, *Cichla orinocensis*, Cichlidae. This fish is much sought after as food, and makes a delicious meal.

perch being all we could muster for supper. As we had the next day to spare, I sent them early to get some 'timbó' to poison the water, and thus obtain some more fish." (WALLACE, 1853B: 244)

"When my Indians returned with the roots of timbó, we all set to work beating it on the rocks with hard pieces of wood, till we had reduced it to fibres. It was then placed in a small canoe, filled with water and clay, well mixed and squeezed, till all the juice had come out of it. This being done, it was carried a little way up the stream, and gradually tilted in, and mixed with the water. It soon began to produce its effects: small fish jumped up out of the water, turned and twisted about on the surface, or – even lay on their backs and sides. The Indians were in the stream with baskets, hooking all that came in the way, and diving and swimming after any larger one that appeared at all affected. In this way, we got in an hour or two a basketful of fish, mostly small ones, but containing many curious species I had not before met with. Numbers escaped, as we had no weir across the stream; and the next day several were found entangled along the sides, and already putrefying. I now had plenty to do. I selected about half-a-dozen of the most novel and interesting species to describe and figure, and gave the rest to be cleaned and put in the pot, to provide us a rather better supper than we had had for some days past." (WALLACE, 1853B: 246–247)

The use of fish poisons is widespread in the tropics. The

chemicals released from pounding the roots of several different types of plants stun or suffocate fishes, enabling them to be caught easily. Many different plants are used as fish poisons in the Amazon. Those used along the Rio Negro and upper Amazon, and called to this day timbó, are usually *Lonchocarpus nicou*, a huge woody vine in the pea family (Fabaceae), and *Paullinia pinnata*, another woody vine in the soapberry family (Sapindaceae). The active chemicals in *Paullinia* are saponins which dissolve easily in water, then irritate mucuous membranes and destroy red blood cells – hence the suffocating effect. Rotenone is the active chemical in *Lonchocarpus* and works in more or less the same way. The beating and crushing of the roots or stems or bark – various parts are used depending on local custom – that Wallace observed helps to release the chemicals, which work quickly once dissolved in the water. Although deadly for the victims, fish caught in this way are perfectly safe for human consumption: the toxic chemicals degrade very quickly. Oddly, many fish poisons are also toxic to insects, and scientists interested in biodegradable pesticides are actively investigating many of these fish poison plants. Rotenone is one compound that has (or had) wide use as an insecticide. Sadly, today the method more often employed to kill fish along rivers and in pools is dynamite. The shock waves from the explosion kill all the fish in the pool where it is used and the dynamite's long-term physical and chemical damage is far more devastating for the local environment than the dramatic, but natural, use of timbó that Wallace observed.

Wallace was amazed by the sheer variety of fishes brought up by fishermen all along the Amazon and into the Rio Negro. Strange forms fascinated him, and he sketched as many fish as he could, recording their shapes and patterning, as well as taking good advantage of always being in the company of local people to record their common names. But it was not always easy. The heat of the tropical sun caused the fish to rot quickly, and as his companions were generally not in the natural history business, he often was not given time to do as much as he wanted. Some of his drawings are oddly inaccurate and in the wrong perspective – due perhaps to sketching under pressure and in a desperate attempt to record as much as possible before the chance was lost.

"One day Senhor Henrique made a party to go fishing, with a large drag net in the Solimões. We started in the afternoon in a good canoe, with a party of about a dozen, and eight or ten Indian rowers; and just before sunset reached the mouth of the Rio Negro, and turned up the strong and turbid waters of the Solimões. There was a bright moon, and we kept talking and singing, while passing the narrow channels and green islands of the north side of the river, which looked most picturesquely wild and solitary, by the pale silvery moonlight, and amid the solemn silence of the forest. Every time the net was drawn on shore, we nearly filled a basket with numerous small fishes, and a few of larger size. There were quantities of little ones armed with spines, which inflict a serious wound if trodden on, so we had to be cautious with our bare feet. I was much interested in the great variety and the curious forms that every basketful contained. There were numbers of a little fish [Amazonian puffer fish], peculiar to the Amazon, which inflates the fore part of the body into a complete ball, and when stamped upon explodes with a noise similar to that produced by the bursting of an inflated paper bag.

Now it was daylight, I endeavoured to sketch some of the curious fish, but they were so numerous, and the sun was so hot, that I could do but little; and as they became putrid in a few hours, I could not keep them for the purpose till we returned home." (WALLACE, 1853B: 190–191)

Arowana, *Osteoglossum bicirrhosum*, Osteoglossidae, Upper Rio Negro. Fish of this species leap high out of the water to catch insects perched on leaves overhanging the water. They are also prized as food.

In recording the various forms and shapes of the fishes he caught, Wallace also thought about how they were related, and sent a paper back to London to be read at the Zoological Society describing what he felt were probably five different genera of fishes related to the electric eel. His careful observations allowed him to see the differences between similar forms and relate this to novelties he was finding in the remote wilds of the Rio Negro. He not only recorded the morphological details of the fishes he collected and sketched, he was interested in their uses and in stories about how they lived, and even more importantly, where they occurred.

"Of all kinds of fishes I found two hundred and five species in the Rio Negro alone, and these, I am sure, are but a small portion of what exist there. Being a black-water river, most of its fishes are different from those found in the Amazon. In fact, in every small river, and in different parts of the same river, distinct kinds are found. The greater part of those which inhabit the Upper Rio Negro are not found near its mouth, where there are many other kinds equally unknown in the clearer, darker, and probably colder waters of its higher branches. From the number of new fishes found in every fresh locality and in every fisherman's basket, we may estimate that at least five hundred species exist in the Rio Negro and its tributary streams. The number in the whole valley of the Amazon, it is impossible to estimate with any approach to accuracy." (WALLACE, 1853B: 467–468)

For Wallace, the sheer numbers of different kinds of species was one of the lures of the Amazon. After all, he and Bates had set off on their great adventure with the express purpose of finding out about "the problem of [the] origin of species". But as he travelled and became more adept at recognising different types of organisms, he also became fascinated by where they occurred – their geographical distributions. He noticed the differences in kinds of fishes in the different tributaries of the Rio Negro and Rio Vaupés as he went further and further from previously explored territory, and he also observed in great detail how features of the environment influenced the distribution of all types of animals. It became with him one of the most important parts of natural history – and it was this fascination with and meticulousness about distribution and range that made him a truly innovative biologist of his day.

"There is no part of natural history more interesting or instructive, than the study of the geographical distribution of animals. It is well known that countries possessing a climate and soil very similar, may differ almost entirely in their productions. … But there must be many other kinds of boundaries besides these [mountain ranges] which, independently of climate, limit the range of animals. Places not more than fifty or a hundred miles apart, often have species of insects and birds at the one, which are not found at the other. There must be some boundary which determines the range of each species; some external peculiarity to mark the line which each one does not pass. Rivers generally do not determine the distribution of species, because when small, there are few animals which cannot pass them; but in very large rivers the case is different, and they will, it is believed, be found to be the limits, determining the range of many animals of all orders. ... With regard to the Amazon and its larger tributaries, I have ascertained this to be the case ..." (WALLACE, 1853B: 469–470)

His time in the field collecting allowed Wallace to observe for himself the distributions of animals, and to begin to think about why they were so. He sent an impassioned plea to the Zoological Society for better recording of locality information. Many earlier collections were so inaccurately labelled and gave so few clues as to where they were from, that from Wallace's point of view they were virtually useless. Collections labelled as from the New World, or from Brazil might contain new species and be interesting for their novelty, but they were with difficulty used to answer biogeographical questions, a fact of which Wallace became acutely aware.

"On this accurate determination of an animal's range many interesting questions depend. Are very closely allied species ever separated by a wide interval of country? What physical features determine the boundaries of species and of genera? Do the isothermal lines ever accurately bound the range of species, or are they altogether independent of them? What are the circumstances which render certain rivers and certain mountain ranges the limits of numerous species, while others not? None of these questions can be satisfactorily answered till we have the range of numerous species accurately determined.

During my residence in the Amazon district I took every opportunity of determining the limits of species, and I soon found that the Amazon, the Rio Negro and the Madeira formed the limits beyond which certain species never passed. The native hunters are perfectly aware of this fact, and always cross over the river when they want to procure certain animals, which are found even on the river's bank on one side, but never by any chance on the other.... In going up the Rio Negro the difference in the two sides of the river is very remarkable. In the lower part of the river you will find on the north the *Jachus bicolor* and the *Brachyurus Couxiu*, and on the south, the red-whiskered *Pithecia*. Higher up you will find on the north the *Ateles paniscus*, and on the south the new black *Jacchus* and the *Lagothrix Humboldtii*.

Spix, in his work on the monkeys of Brazil, frequently gives, "banks of the river Amazon" as a locality, not being aware that the species found on one side do not very often occur on the other, though the fact is generally known to the natives. In these observations I have only referred to the monkeys, but the phænomena occur with both

birds and insects, as I have observed in many instances."
(WALLACE, 1852B: 109–110)

These studies of the facts and patterns of species distribution are the science of biogeography. Natural scientists are always interested in the questions of where and who – what species occur in which parts of the earth's surface. Wallace was also uniquely interested in the why. His great skill at seeing patterns and in linking isolated pieces of observation into a coherent whole made him the first real evolutionary biogeographer – he applied distribution data for plants and animals to the "problem of [the] origin of species". To do that one needs collections – lots of them. These he set about obtaining in the Amazon, always thinking about previous observations and comparing them to his own.

But the true flowering of Wallace's thinking on biogeography was to come later, in the Malay Archipelago, where Wallace's line, the great dividing line between the Asian and the Australian faunas, commemorates his obsession with the where, the who and the why. Events overtook him in the Amazon, and the loss of his collections precluded any detailed analysis, much to his intense disappointment.

"Of the smaller perching birds and insects, which doubtless would have afforded many interesting facts corroborative of those already mentioned, I have nothing to say, as my extensive collection of specimens from the

Rio Negro and Upper Amazon, all ticketed for my own use, have been lost; and of course in such a question as this, the exact determination of species is everything." (WALLACE, 1853B: 473–474)

But all the time he was thinking about the big questions, Wallace was collecting novelties for sale back in London, and having the time of his life.

"Besides the umbrella birds, the little bristle-tailed manakin will, I think be good; also the trumpeter, which is a species different from that at Pará; the muscovy ducks also. Both among birds and insects there are, I know, many common as well as rare species. There are also two bad specimens of the celebrated "bell bird", which I believe is rare; they frequent the highest trees out of ordinary gun-shot; my hunter fired five or six times at each of them, and after several ineffectual shots at another gave it up in despair. Of the curl-crested araçari, I have only at present got a single specimen. The araçaris I send are two species new to me, and both much prettier than the curl-crested." (WALLACE, 1850B: 496)

It seems strange to us now to kill birds to identify them – these days we have access to the most wonderful illustrated field guides to the birds of many parts of the world, which allow us to use our binoculars to hunt rare and exciting birdlife, instead of a gun as did Wallace.

But in Wallace's day, very little was known scientifically about the birds of the tropics and that only from the few specimens which made it back to European and American collections. In the Amazon Wallace would have collected as many specimens of birds as he could shoot, some for sale and others for his own personal collection. Only by examining a large number of individuals does the variety of species and variability within a single species become apparent. But enough was known about the oddities of birds in the Amazon basin for Wallace to set off in search of particular species such as the spectacular umbrella bird, said to be found along the Rio Negro.

"The wet season had now set in, and we soon found there was little to be done in collecting birds or insects at Barra. I had been informed that this was the time to find the celebrated umbrella chatterers in plumage, and that they were plentiful in the islands about three days' voyage up the Rio Negro …

The birds are tolerably abundant, but shy…. My hunter worked very perseveringly to get them, going out before daylight and often not returning till nine or ten at night, yet he never brought me more than two at a time, generally only one, and sometimes none." (WALLACE, 1853B: 165–170)

In addition to collecting as many individuals as he could, Wallace kept one of the birds in a cage for ten days until it suddenly died, and closely observed its behaviour and how the peculiar structures for which it is named functioned.

Astrocaryum gynacanthum.

Mumbáca, *Astrocaryum gynacanthum.* "This species has a rather slender stem ..., covered with long, flat, black spines, arranged in regular rings and pointing downwards."

"The Umbrella Bird is about the size of a crow, averaging about 18 inches in length. Its colour is entirely black, but varied with metallic blue tints on the outer margin of its feathers…. Were it not for its crest and neck plume it would appear to an ordinary observer nothing more than a short-legged crow.

The crest is perhaps the most fully developed and most beautiful of any bird known. It is composed of long slender feathers, rising from a contractile skin on the top of the head. The shafts are white and the plume glossy blue, hair-like and curved outward at the tip. When the crest is laid back the shafts form a compact white mass, sloping up from the top of the head, and surmounted by the dense hairy plumes. Even in this position it is not an inelegant crest, but it is when it is fully opened that its peculiar character is developed. The shafts then radiate on all sides from the tip of the head, reaching in front beyond and below the top of the beak, which is completely hid from view. The top then forms a perfect, slightly elongated dome, of a beautiful shining blue colour, having a point of divergence rather behind the centre, like that in the human head. The length of this dome from front to back is about 5 inches, the breadth 4 to 4½ inches. The other singular appendage of this bird is the neck plume. This is a long cylindrical plume of feathers depending from the middle of the neck, and either carried close to the breast or puffed out and hanging down in front. The feathers lap over each other, scale-like, and are bordered with fine metallic blue.

When in motion, either flying or feeding, the crest is laid back and the plume carried close to the breast, so as not to be conspicuous. When at rest in the day-time, the crest is fully expanded, and the plume is rather enlarged and hanging forward. At night, when asleep, the feathers are puffed out to their fullest extent, and sometimes the head is turned so as to bring the dome of the crest on the middle of the back. It then presents a most singular appearance, the head and feet being quite invisible, the plume and crest alone being conspicuous amidst the mass of feathers…. Its note is very loud and deep, and it is from this that it has received its Indian name 'Ueramimbé', signifying the 'Piper-bird'. It utters its note very early in the morning and in the afternoon. It frequents the very loftiest forest trees …" (WALLACE, 1850c: 206–207)

Although it looks like a large, short-legged crow, the umbrella bird is really a member of the cotinga family. The cotingas are exclusively South and Central American, and are among the most diverse of all bird families. The umbrella bird is the largest species in the group, but it is by no means the most peculiarly ornamented. Cotingas may be the most spectacular of the birds in the American tropics and for sheer exuberance of colour and ornamentation they are second only to the famed birds of paradise of Southeast Asia – in which Wallace became deeply interested during his fieldwork in the Malay Archipelago. As Wallace ascended the Rio Negro, further and further into unknown territory, and through more and more dangerous and tricky situations, he decided to go in search of another spectacular cotinga, the cock-of-the-rock.

The cock-of-the-rock is a strange looking bird. The females are drab and greenish brown, hardly worth noticing. The males are another matter: the body is covered with bright orange, almost luminescent feathers, interrupted only by the strikingly striped, black and white wings and tail. The feathers near the wings are long and silky, but the oddest part of the bird's plumage is the crest. Extending forward and completely overlapping the beak, it is stiff and laterally compressed, and is reminiscent of ornament on a Roman legionnaire's helmet. Such a peculiarly ornamented bird was bound to be prized by collectors back in England. To get to the upper Rio Negro, and these amazing birds, Wallace had to ascend the celebrated falls of the Rio Negro. This took him four days and was not without exciting incident.

"Beds and ledges of rock spread all across the river, while through the openings between them water rushed with terrific violence, forming dangerous whirlpools and breakers below. Here it was necessary to cross to the other side, in order to get up. We dashed into the current, were rapidly carried down, got among the boiling waves, then passed suddenly into still water under shelter of an island; whence starting again, we at length reached the other side, about a mile across …

As we went on we constantly encountered fresh difficulties. Sometimes we had to cross into the middle of the stream, to avoid some impassable mass of rocks; at others, the canoe was dragged and pushed in narrow channels, that hardly allowed it to pass. The Indians, all naked, with their trousers tied around their loins, plunged about in the water like fishes. Sometimes a projecting crag had to be reached with a tow-rope. An Indian takes it in his hand, and leaps into the rapid current: he is carried down by its irresistible force. Now he dives to the bottom,

"Channel among Granite rocks, Rio Negro above St. Jozé Nov 51."

and there swims and crawls along, where the stream has less power. After two or three trials, he reaches the rock, and tries to mount upon it; but it rises high and abruptly out of the water, and after several efforts he falls back exhausted, and floats down again to the canoe amid the mirth and laughter of his comrades. Another now tries, with the same result. Then another plunges in without the rope, and thus unencumbered mounts on the rock and gives a helping hand to his companion; and then all go to work, and we are pulled up past the obstacle …

I can see no escape, but in a moment we are in an eddy caused by a sunken mass above us; again we go on, and reach at length our object, a rocky island, round which we pull and push our canoe, and from the upper point cross to another, and so make a zigzag course, until, after some hours' hard work, we at length reach the bank, perhaps not fifty yards above the obstacle which had obliged us to leave it." (WALLACE, 1853B: 205–207)

Above the rapids the Rio Negro again became calm, placid and black as night. The famed cocks-of-the-rock were not to be found close to any of the tiny villages Wallace stayed in, but were said to come from lonely granite mountains up a tributary of the main river, the Cobatí. Wallace borrowed a small canoe and with his two hunters, set off in search of the birds. Up the Cobatí he found himself far away from the semi-European civilisation he had hitherto been a part of. Here the people spoke not a word of Portuguese and barely even conversed in the "lingoa geral" – the common language spoken along the Amazon – but were amazingly in tune with the forest and its creatures.

"But Indian boys are not great talkers, and a few monosyllables would generally suffice for our communication. One or two of them had blow-pipes, and shot numbers of small birds for me, while others would creep along by my side and silently point out birds, or small animals, before I could catch sight of them. When I fired, and, as was often the case, the bird flew away wounded, they would bound away after it, and seldom search in vain ...

... I soon found that the Cocks of the Rock, to obtain which was my chief object in coming here, were not to be found near the village. Their principal resort was the Serra de Cobáti, or mountain before mentioned, situated some ten or twelve miles off in the forest, where I was informed they were very abundant. I accordingly made arrangements for a trip to the Serra, and with the intention of staying there for a week. By promise of good payment for every 'Gallo' they killed for me, I persuaded almost the whole male population of the village to accompany me. As our path was through a dense forest for ten miles, we could not load ourselves with much baggage: every man had to carry his gravatána [blowpipe], bow and arrows, rede [hammock], and some farinha; which with salt, was all the provisions we took, trusting to the forest for our meat; and I even gave up my daily and only luxury of coffee." (WALLACE, 1853B: 214–216)

They soon left even isolated houses behind, and the men killed all their meat along the way with blow-pipes and poisoned arrows. The blowpipes and poisoned arrows of South American peoples are legendary. They were first described by the Spanish conquistadores with amazement – imagine a tiny, needle-like arrow that caused death instantly! The blowpipe, or gravataná, itself can be up to two metres long and it is made from the carefully hollowed stems of palms, reeds or bamboos, depending on local custom. The stem is split carefully in half, bored out extremely accurately and then reassembled into a tube, bound together with cotton thread or strips of bark. The accuracy with which prey can be shot is directly dependent upon the straightness of the tube – and for this reason the best blowpipes are much treasured possessions. The arrows are tiny, about ten to twenty centimetres long, and made from slivers of very hard palm stem made needle-sharp at the tip. The back of the arrow is packed into kapok fluff, against which the hunter blows to expel the arrow from the tube. The lethal effect of the arrows is caused by a variety of poisons applied to the fragile, needle-sharp tips. In the Rio Negro region the commonly used poison is curare. Made from a complex mixture of plant barks, it was first described by Father Cristóbal de Acuña, a Spanish priest who wrote about early explorations of the Amazon in a book published in

1641. The main components were not identified until the early 1800s, and each group of people who used curare had a slightly different recipe. The active ingredients for most curares come from various species of *Strychnos* in the logania family (Loganiaceae), and *Chondrodendron* in the moonseed family (Menispermaceae) – both these plants are large, woody vines from primary forests. The potent chemicals in the mixture are strong, smooth muscle relaxants and also affect the nervous system – hence their lethal effect upon the hapless animals targeted by blowpipes! Curare is still in use today, not so much in the Amazon, but in modern medicine, especially in abdominal surgery.

"Serras of Curicuriari" along the Rio Vaupés.

Even though he still preferred his gun to the native blowpipes, Wallace had adapted to local practices to some extent. He shed his boots and went barefoot even on long treks such as this one, but still his passage through the forest was not easy and silent like that of the villagers accompanying him.

"Hard roots rose up in ridges along our path, swamp and mud alternated with quartz pebbles and rotten leaves; and as I floundered along in bare-footed enjoyment of these, some overhanging bough would knock my cap from my head or the gun from my hand; or the hooked spines of the climbing palms would catch in my shirt-sleeves, and oblige me either to halt and deliberately unhook myself, or leave a portion of the unlucky garment behind. The Indians were all naked, or, if they had shirt and trowsers, carried them in a bundle on their heads, and I have no doubt looked on me as a good illustration of the uselessness and bad consequences of wearing clothes upon a forest journey." (WALLACE, 1853B: 217–218)

The journey into the mountains was extremely difficult, and the terrain very steep and rugged. Although from the air the forest cover makes such an area look smooth, the ground underneath is as jagged as a saw blade. The bird that Wallace was seeking was the Guianan cock-of-the-rock, one of two species of cocks-of-the rock, the other species occurs in the Andes and has completely different behaviour and nesting habits. The nest of the Guianan cock-of-the-rock is a solid bracket of mud and bits of plant fixed to a vertical rock face – thus the bird's restricted distribution in such rough and remote granitic mountains. We have probably all seen nests like this built by house martins or barn swallows – these birds are 4–6 cm long and weigh about 17 g – but imagine such a structure being used by a bird about 16 or 17 cm long and weighing more than 100 g. Wallace never saw the females of this bird, but that was hardly surprising; he was after the brilliantly plumaged males, not the drab, brown females.

"All the time we kept a sharp look-out, but saw no birds. At length however an old Indian caught hold of my arm, and whispering gently, "Gallo!" pointed into a dense thicket. After looking intently a little while, I caught a glimpse of the magnificent bird sitting amidst the gloom, shining out like a mass of brilliant flame. … In a few minutes however it was brought to me, and I was lost in admiration of the dazzling brilliancy of its soft downy feathers. … They [the birds] are caught by snares at certain places, where the males assemble to play. These are places on racks, or roots of trees, and are worn quite smooth and clean. Two or three males meet and perform a kind of dance, walking and jigging up and down. The females and young are never seen at these places, so that you are sure of catching only full-grown fine-plumaged males." (WALLACE, 1853B: 221–227)

In a stay of nine days in the mountains, Wallace and his hunters obtained twelve cocks-of-the-rock and several

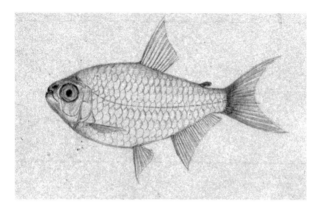

Moenkhausia oligolepis, Characidae, Rio Vaupés.

Matapirí, *Heterocharax virgulatus,* Characidae, Upper Rio Negro.

Crenuchus spilurus, Crenuchidae, sources of Rio Negro. These fish are very popular in the aquarium trade, but are quite territorial and extremely aggressive.

A small species of the incredibly diverse family Characidae, the characins. Upper Rio Negro.

other species of rare and interesting birds. All this killing may seem excessive to us but to Wallace it was a way of documenting what he saw. There were very few specimens of these magnificent birds in collections and very little was known about them. Even their peculiar and spectacular courtship displays were not described in detail until the 1960s. The communal dancefloors described by Wallace, and before him seen by Schomburgk, were variously interpreted as places where males danced for each other, or where males took turns dancing for females who were watching. In reality, each male has a small patch on the communal dancefloor where he displays with his crest and extraordinary wing feathers for watching females, trying to entice them to mate with him.

Some early collectors were so intent upon the acquisition of specimens that they shot first and asked questions afterwards. But Wallace was not one of these sorts of collectors – although he did his share of getting the best specimens for sale back in England. He keenly and carefully observed the behaviour of animals in the wild and sometimes was so stunned by their beauty and sheer perfection that he held his fire.

"As I was walking quietly along I saw a large, jet-black animal come out of the forest about twenty yards before me, and which took me so much by surprise that I did not at all imagine what it was. As it moved slowly on, and its whole body and long curving tail came into view in the middle of the road, I saw that it was a fine black jaguar. I involuntarily raised my gun to my shoulder, but remembering that both barrels were loaded with small shot, and that to fire would exasperate without killing him, I stood silently gazing. In the middle of the road he turned his head, and for an instant paused and gazed on me, but having, I suppose, other business of his own to attend to, walked steadily on, and disappeared in the thicket. ... This encounter pleased me very much. I was too much surprised, and occupied too much with admiration, to feel fear. I had at length had a full view, in his native wilds, of the rarest variety of the most powerful and dangerous animal inhabiting the American continent." (WALLACE, 1853B: 241–242)

An encounter with a jaguar is a magical experience. To most people they epitomise the wild, untamed nature of the tropical rainforest, and it is not at all surprising that Wallace stood and gazed. Three years after setting out from England to explore and collect in the Amazon, high up the Rio Negro in Venezuela, having explored places and seen things no other collector had seen, Wallace truly felt himself "Rich without wealth, happy without gold!" (WALLACE, 1853B: 261, POEM WRITTEN IN JAVITA, MARCH 1851)

Mammals are not easily seen in the American tropics;

Jará assú, *Leopoldinia major.* "This tree occurs plentifully on the lakes and inlets of the upper Rio Negro, but is not found at the mouth of the river ... [it is] often found with a part of the stem under water."

it is not like the plains of Africa where great herds of mammals are seen wherever one looks. This often disappoints the visitor to the rainforest, who expects to see animals in their wild state everywhere. Most mammals in the New World tropics are secretive and often nocturnal. Wallace was extremely fortunate to see a jaguar in broad daylight, and a naturalist today would be even more fortunate. As suitable habitat is destroyed, and more and more people with guns hunt in the forests, the mammals become rarer and more shy, and much harder to see. Wallace felt that "the Amazon valley is remarkably deficient in large animals" (WALLACE, 1853B: 446) but he made an exception for the monkeys, which were plentiful enough for him to observe in numbers.

"… but almost the only animals found in any numbers are the monkeys, which are abundant, both in species and individuals, and are the only mammalia that give some degree of life to these trackless forests, which seem peculiarly fitted for their development and increase." (WALLACE, 1853B: 447)

In his travels Wallace observed twenty-one species of monkeys, ranging from the tiny marmosets to the large howlers to the docile and gentle woolly monkeys of the upper Rio Negro. His first encounter with a monkey was one of the great excitements of the start of his travels, and really made him feel he was in the tropics, beginning a great adventure.

"But to me the greatest treat was making my first

Mucuja, *Acrocomia aculeata*. "Common in the neighbourhood of Pará, where its globular crown of drooping feathery leaves is very ornamental. The fruit, though oily and bitter, is very much esteemed and is eagerly sought after."

acquaintance with the monkeys. One morning, when walking alone in the forest, I heard a rustling of the leaves and branches, as if a man were walking quickly among them, and expected every minute to see some Indian hunter make his appearance, when all at once the sounds appeared to be in the branches above, and turning up my eyes there, I saw a large monkey looking down at me, and seeming as much astonished as I was myself ... At last one approached too near for its safety. Mr. Leavens fired, and it fell, the rest making off with all possible speed. The poor little animal was not quite dead, and its cries, its innocent looking countenance, and delicate little hands were quite childlike." (WALLACE, 1853B: 41–42)

Howler monkeys are among the most extraordinary of the New World monkeys – mostly for their astoundingly loud vocalisations. Wallace observed and collected what he thought were three species of howler monkeys, in varying shades of black and red. These monkeys are extremely variable in colour, but all howlers are sexually dimorphic; the males and females being very different. The males have a blackish beard and an enlarged, swollen throat and it is from here that the incredibly loud roars come. When a male howler is roaring it can be heard for miles. Choruses are usually heard in the early morning or late in the afternoon, and often when it is about to rain. The roaring is started by a single male, with a series of deep grunts, which then accelerate into long, deep roars. Other individuals, both male and female, join in and the ensuing cacophony is unbelievable – especially if one happens to be quite close by. The great explorer Humboldt felt that such a noise could only be made by a large number of animals roaring together simultaneously, but Wallace realised he was at least partly wrong, and was not shy about showing it.

"Humboldt observes, that the tremendous noise they make can only be accounted for by the great numbers of individuals that unite in its production. My own observations, and the unanimous testimony of the Indians, prove this not to be the case. One individual only makes the howling, which is certainly of a remarkable depth and volume and curiously modulated; but on closely remarking the suddenness with which it ceases and again commences, it is evident that it is produced by one animal, which is generally a full-grown male. On dissecting the throat, much of our wonder at the noise ceases; for besides the bony vessel formed by the expanded "os hyoides", there is a strong muscular apparatus which seems to act as a bellows in forcing a body of air through the reverberating bony cavity." (WALLACE, 1852B: 107–108)

Wallace not only collected monkeys, he observed their distributions carefully. Monkeys were among the animals that led him to speculate on the reasons for distributional difference and the barriers to migration. He also kept some monkeys as pets, and tried to bring several woolly monkeys back to England alive, but failed through no fault of his own.

"They [*Lagothrix humboldtii*, now *Lagothrix lagothricha*] are remarkable for their thick woolly grey fur, their long prehensile tails, and very mild disposition. In the upper Amazon they are the species most frequently seen tame, and are great favourites, from their grave countenances, more resembling the human face than those of other Monkeys, their quiet manners, and the great affection and docility they exhibit. I had three of them for several months before leaving Brazil, and they were on board with me at the time the ship was burnt, when, with their companions, they all perished." (WALLACE, 1852B: 108)

The woolly monkeys Wallace saw and kept were the common species, and at the time were found all over the upper Amazon basin. Woolly monkeys are indeed very human-like, and are still much prized as pets by local people. However they are now intensively hunted and are locally extinct in many parts of the Amazon basin as they are considered to be the most tasty of all the monkey species. Habitat destruction is also reducing the forest patches where these monkeys live. The other species in this genus is extremely rare and endangered. The yellow-tailed woolly monkey was discovered in Colombia by Humboldt in 1802, then next seen in the 1920s. It was afterwards thought to be extinct, but in the 1970s was rediscovered in a small, remote area of eastern Peru. Conservation efforts involving the local communities are helping to conserve its habitat and to highlight it as important for more than just its food value.

The people of the Amazon were, and still are, extremely knowledgeable about the animals and plants occurring in their district. Wallace, rather than assuming he knew best because he was a naturalist, took full advantage of the help people were willing to give him. The people he met along the Amazon were amazingly diverse and Wallace observed them with a naturalist's eye.

"The inhabitants of Pará, as of all Brazil, consist of three distinct races: the Portuguese and their descendants with a few other Europeans, the native Indians, and the Negroes together with a considerable number of mixed descent. The Indians in and near Pará are all 'tame Indians', being Roman Catholics in religion and speaking Portuguese, though many also speak the Lingoa-Geral or common Indian language. They are the chief boatmen, fishermen, hunters, and cultivators in the country, while many of them work as labourers or mechanics in the towns. The negroes were originally all slaves, but a large number are now free, some having purchased their freedom, while others have been freed by their owners by gift or by will … The people of all races are universally polite, and are generally temperate and peaceful." (WALLACE, 1905: 273, LETTER TO THE MECHANICS INSTITUTION OF NEATH)

Networks of European settlers were very important to Wallace as the means to introduce him to others who could accompany him on journeys further and further

Caraná, *Mauritia carana*. "This is a large smooth-stemmed species allied to *M[auritia] flexuosa*, but quite distinct and hitherto undescribed."

into the interior. Letters of introduction he carried from W. H. Edwards and others back in England gave him the legitimacy necessary to enable him to carry out his collecting with relative ease. But, despite this, he was exasperated with some of the customs of the country, and with the behaviour of many of the people he met as he went on his way.

"… just as I was going, [he] requested me, as a favour, to tell everybody that I had not found him at his sitio, but that he was gone to the 'mato' to get salsa. As I was already on familiar terms with him, I told him that really I was very sorry I could not oblige him, but that, as I was not accustomed to lying, I should be found out immediately if I attempted it: he however insisted that I might surely

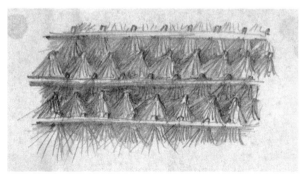

Roof thatch made from the leaves of caraná. "A roof well-thatched with Caraná will last eight or ten years without renewing, the leaves are so constantly cut for this purpose that it is hardly possible to find an entire handsome tree."

Jacitára, *Desmoncus polyacanthos*. A climber, which with backwards-pointing hooks goes high into the canopy; it can cause problems for a naturalist on the forest floor hooking into clothes or nets. "Woe then to the impatient wanderer! A pull or tug will inevitably cause a portion of the fractured garment to stay behind for the "jacitara" never looses its hold…"

try, and I should soon learn to lie as well as the best of them. So I told him at once, that in my country a liar was considered as bad as a thief; at which he seemed rather astonished. I gave him a short account of the pillory, as a proof of how much our ancestors detested lying and perjury, which much edified him, and he called his son (a nice boy of twelve or fourteen, just back from school), to hear and profit from the example; showing I think, that the people here are perfectly aware of the moral enormity of the practice, but that constant habit and universal custom, and above, the false politeness which renders them unable to verbally deny anything, has rendered it almost a necessary evil." (WALLACE, 1853B: 333)

"Truth in fact, in matters of business is so seldom made use of, that a lie seems preferred even when it can serve no purpose whatever, and where the person addressed must be perfectly aware of the falsehood of every asseveration made; but Portuguese politeness does not permit him by word or look to throw any doubt on his friend's veracity. I have often been amused to hear two parties endeavouring to cheat each other, by assertions which each party knew to be perfectly false, and yet pretended to receive as undoubted fact." (WALLACE, 1853B: 381)

"It is this universal love of trade which leads, I think, to three great vices very prevalent here – drinking, gambling, and lying – besides a whole host of trickeries, cheatings and debaucheries of every description." (WALLACE, 1853B: 380)

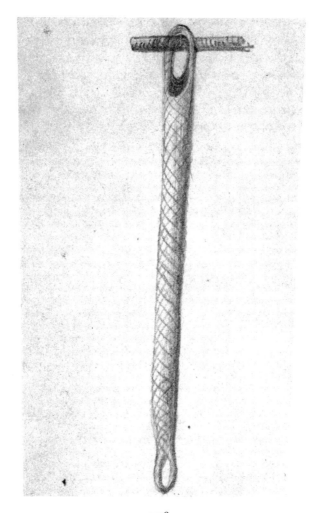

But although Wallace saw much in Brazilian society to irritate him, he generally got on well with his fellow human beings, and had many good times in the company of strange companions. He cheerfully recounts stories of the priest, "a tall, thin prematurely old man, thoroughly worn out by every debauchery" (WALLACE, 1853B: 228), who never told the same tall tale twice, and never got up to any mischief *during the day*, and of Senhor Henrique of Barra, who unfailing helped Wallace obtain canoes and men to paddle further and further upriver. Some people he met, such as Senhor José Antonio Brandão who had a farm on the Solimões just above Barra, made him think about how lucky he himself was, and how his life, though difficult and not one of wealthy ease, was in fact quite fortunate.

"He is a remarkably intelligent man, fond of reading, but without books, and with a most tenacious memory. … He has several huge quarto volumes of Ecclesiastical

Tipití, or cassava strainer. The tube, sometimes up to two metres long, is usually woven from bark or jacitára. To make farinha, the staple starchy food of the Amazon, grated cassava is put into the long tube of the tipití, whch is usually suspended from the roof beams of the house. A person sits on a lever inserted through the bottom loop, compressing the wet, grated cassava so that the liquid is completely extracted, thus ridding the material of toxic cyanides. The resulting meal is dried over the fire in large, earthen plates, making farinha, which keeps well and weighs little, perfect food for travellers.

Cassava grater and flat earthenware griddle for making farinha.

History, and is quite learned in all the details of the Councils, and in the history of the Reformation. He can tell you, from an old work on geography, without maps, the length and breadth of every country in Europe, and the main particulars respecting it. He is about seventy years of age, thirsting for information, and has never seen a map! Think of this, all ye who roll in intellectual luxury. In this land of mechanics' institutions and cheap literature few have an idea of the real pursuit of knowledge under difficulties, of the longing thirst for information which there is no fountain to satisfy." (WALLACE, 1853B: 188)

This thirst for knowledge is part of being human. Today, in remote, and even in not so remote, parts of the Amazon, plant collectors, who these days use newspapers in which to press their specimens, are begged to leave one or two of these papers behind, even if they are very out of date. Many people in the remoter parts of the country have seen no written news for months – and despite the widespread use of the radio, there is a pleasure in being able to read and gain knowledge from the written word. The curiosity with which collectors of all types are greeted in small, out-of-the-way villages is another symptom of this quest for knowledge. People are endlessly fascinated by the antics of naturalists as they go about their daily tasks. What are they doing? Why do they press the flowers between sheets of newspaper? Why do they want that little insignificant insect when there are lovely butterflies for the taking? A collector preparing his or her specimens

Caruru pira miri, *Characidium declivirostre*, Characidae,
Rio Vaupés.

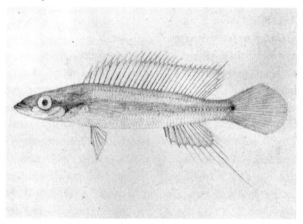

Crenicichla notophthalmus, Cichlidae. This fish was named in
honour of Wallace and his drawing was the type; unfortunately it
had a name already, by which it is now known.

can be the focus for community entertainment in places without television. Imagine a group of completely silent watchers, eyeing your every move as you press plants by candlelight. The occasional whisper or question from a child is the only sound. It can be eerie, but is the ideal opportunity to interact with people and to get to know them better. Wallace was also watched intently by people as he travelled the Amazon. Some things never change!

"While preparing insects or skinning birds in the house, the window which opened into the street was generally crowded with boys and men, who would wait for hours, watching my operations with the most untiring curiosity. The constantly repeated remark, on seeing a bird skinned, was, "Oh, the patience of the whites!" Then one would whisper to another, "Does he take all the meat out?" "Well I never!" "Look, he makes eyes of cotton!" And then would come a little conversation as to what they could possibly be wanted for. "Para mostrar" (to show) was the general solution; but they seemed to think it rather unsatisfactory, and that the English could hardly be such fools as to want to see a few parrot and pigeon skins. The butterflies they settled much to their own satisfaction, deciding that they were for the purpose of obtaining new patterns for printed calicoes and other goods while the ugly insects were supposed to be valuable for "remedios," or medicine." (WALLACE, 1853B: 61)

He also thought deeply about the human condition, not surprising for a man who back in England had been introduced to the principles of Robert Owen, the great utopian socialist. For Owen, each man was an individual, and the product of circumstance. The essential unity of mankind was the means of progressive improvement, largely through education and the acquisition of knowledge. Although Wallace clearly saw the differences in the people he came across in his travels, he thought about how they were situated and if that were right and proper. When he stayed with a large plantation owner who still kept slaves on the lower Amazon, he wondered if the system of slavery was truly for the best, even though all the physical and moral needs of the slaves were taken care of by the enlightened owner, who never separated man from wife, parents from children, and who treated them well in sickness and in health.

"But looking at it in this, its most favourable light, can we say that slavery is good or justifiable? Can it be right to keep a number of our fellow-creatures in a state of adult infancy, of unthinking childhood? It is the responsibility and self-defence of manhood that calls forth the highest powers and energies of our race. It is the struggle for existence, the 'battle for life', which exercises the moral faculties and calls forth the latent sparks of genius. The hope of gain, the love of power, the desire of fame and approbation, excite to noble deeds, and call into action all those faculties which are the distinctive attributes of man.

Childhood is the animal part of man's existence, manhood the intellectual; and when the weakness and imbecility of childhood remain, without its simplicity and pureness, its grace and beauty, how degrading is the spectacle! And this is the state of the slave when slavery is the best it can be." (WALLACE, 1853B: 121)

But it was the native peoples of the Amazon who most struck Wallace. Although in his writings he speaks of them all as Indians, he was very careful to record where they lived and what they called themselves. He details the names of the groups living up the Rio Vaupés and upper Rio Negro, and he constantly expresses admiration for their skills and their knowledge of the forest.

"I have myself had opportunities of observing the Aborigines of the interior, in places where they retain all their native customs and peculiarities. These truly uncivilized Indians are seen by few travellers, and can only be found by going far beyond the dwellings of white men, and out of the ordinary track of trade. In the neighbourhood of civilization the Indian loses many of his peculiar customs, changes his mode of life, his house, his costume, and his language, becomes imbued with the prejudices of civilization, and adopts the forms and ceremonies of the Roman Catholic religion. In this state he is a different being from the true denizen of the forests, and it may be doubted, where his civilization goes no further than this, if he is not a degenerated and degraded one; but it is in this state alone that he is met with by most travellers in Brazil, on the banks of the Amazon…" (WALLACE, 1853B: 476–477)

Most of these "tame Indians" spoke the lingoa geral, a sort of general language devised by the Jesuits to enable the differing groups with widely divergent languages to communicate with each other and with traders who moved up and down the rivers and in and out of different language groups. It is based on the Tupi language, and Wallace, in addition to his knowledge of Portuguese, learned to speak it very well when he was in Brazil. This served him well when he went into Venezuela where Spanish, and not Portuguese, was spoken. As he went further and further up the Rio Negro and then up the Rio Vaupés, he encountered more villages where nothing but the local language was spoken, and he began to collect words and construct vocabularies of Amazonian languages. In his first edition (1853) of *Travels on the Amazon*, he compiled a synonymy of 98 words with their equivalents in English, lingoa geral and ten different native languages. This compilation was, sadly, left out of the re-issue (1889) of the book as perhaps not being of interest to the general reader. In addition to collecting specimens of natural history and words from unknown languages, Wallace also collected artefacts manufactured by local people as he travelled and recorded local customs.

"There are two painted calabashes in paper with your

name outside; please accept them as a specimen of the Indian girls' work at Montealegre; the varnish, colours, &c., are all made by themselves from the leaves and bark of different trees and herbs; they paint them with bits of stick and feathers, and the patterns are all their own design; they are the usual drinking vessels here, but less ornamented from common use." (WALLACE, 1850B: 495)

As he travelled further and further into the interior, up the Rio Vaupés, Wallace encountered more and more native peoples living in harmony with their surroundings and untroubled by 'civilised' life.

"It was the men however who presented the most novel appearance, as different from all the half-civilized races among whom I had been so long living, as they could be if I had been suddenly transported to another quarter of the globe. Their hair was carefully parted in the middle, combed behind the ears, and tied behind them in a long tail reaching a yard down the back. The hair of this tail was firmly bound with a long cord formed of monkey's hair, very soft and pliable. On the top of the head was stuck a comb, ingeniously constructed of palm-wood and grass, and ornamented with little tufts of toucans' rump feathers at each end; and the ears were pierced, and a small piece of straw stuck in the hole; altogether giving a most feminine appearance to the face, increased by the total absence of beard or whiskers, and by the hair of the eyebrows being almost entirely plucked out." (WALLACE, 1853B: 277)

This far up the Rio Vaupés, near the falls, the people did not speak the lingoa geral as fluently as further down the river, but still Wallace managed to fit in. He was invited to a celebration – where the inhabitants of several family groups got together for a night of dancing and revelry. He saw the preparation of caxiri, a fermented beer made from cassava roots, and witnessed, but did not try, the famed narcotic caapí, also known as yagé or ayahuasca in the upper Amazon basin. This drug has been the subject of many adventures of naturalists, from Wallace and Spruce to the present day. It is made from a mixture of several plants, the most important of which is the woody vine *Banisteriopsis caapi*, in the family Malphigiaceae. An infusion of the bark is prepared and drunk by the shaman and those involved in the ceremony; the effects are amazing. A violent purgative and emetic, it also induces floods of visions, often of colour and shape. Everything beautiful or wonderful is said to pass before your eyes and the whole world pulsates. Music is an essential part of the caapí drinking ceremony, and the shaman uses music to direct and control the experience. The visions put the shaman and all who partake in touch with the spirit world. The use of caapí is very important for the peoples of the upper Amazon as a way to keep in tune with the

Artefacts sketched by Wallace along the Rio Vaupés. Combs worn in men's hair during celebrations were tipped with brilliantly coloured toucan feathers. In the Amazon, small canoes are often made from a single tree trunk.

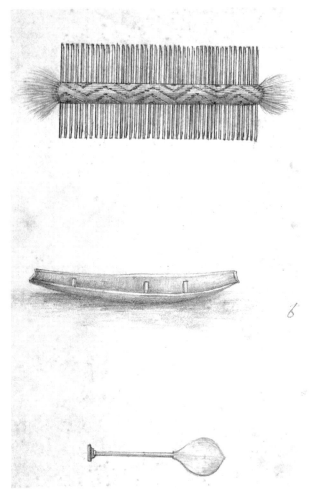

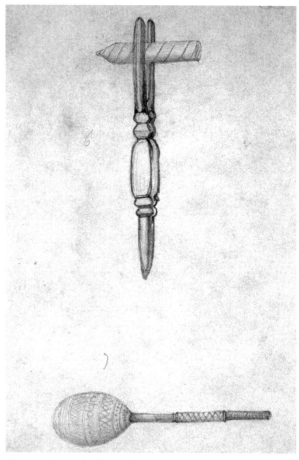

Ceremonial cigar holder and musical rattle, sketched by Wallace along the Rio Vaupés.

world that has been before and the world that now exists around them. The mixtures of other plants in the infusion serve to enhance the visions – making them stronger and more intense. Wallace was invited to a ceremony, but did not partake of the infusion himself. About a year later, Wallace's great friend Richard Spruce did accept some of the infusion in a similar ceremony along the Rio Vaupés. He only managed a half of the dose, then felt very nauseous indeed. Perhaps Wallace had been well advised to forego the pleasure.

At the same feast Wallace was also offered a puff on a giant cigar, which was held in a huge cigar holder stuck in the ground while not in use. He seems to have passed that opportunity up as well, but sketched the cigar and its holder, along with other artefacts he saw in the communal houses along the Rio Vaupés.

"The wild and strange appearance of these handsome, naked, painted Indians, with their curious ornaments and weapons, the stamp and song and rattle which accompanies the dance, the hum of conversation in a strange language, the music of fifes and flutes and other instruments of reed, bone, and turtles' shells, the large calabashes of caxirí constantly carried about, and the great smoke-blackened gloomy house, produced an effect to which no description can do justice, and of which the sight of half-a-dozen Indians going through their dance for show, gives but a very faint idea." (WALLACE, 1853B: 282)

Above the falls of the Rio Vaupés, further up that river than any European had penetrated thus far, Wallace became the first Westerner to record the legend of the Yuriparí – and to witness the making of 'devil-music'.

"One evening there was a caxirí-drinking; and a little before dusk, a sound of trombones and bassoons was heard coming on the river towards the village, and presently appeared eight Indians, each playing on a great bassoon-looking instrument. They had four pairs, of different sizes, and produced a wild and pleasing sound. They blew them all together, tolerably in concert, to a simple tune, and showed more taste for music

Malocca, a communal dwelling roofed with palm thatch, on the Rio Vaupés.

than I had yet seen displayed among these people. The instruments are made of bark spirally twisted, and with a mouthpiece of leaves. ... In the evening I went to the malocca, and found two old men playing on the largest of the instruments. They waved them about in a singular manner, vertically and sideways, accompanied by corresponding contortions of the body, and played a long while in a regular tune, accompanying each other very correctly. From the moment the music was first heard, not a female, old or young, was to be seen; for it is one of the strangest superstitions of the Uaupés Indians, that they consider it so dangerous for a woman ever to see one of their instruments, that having done so is punished with death, generally by poison. Even should the view be perfectly accidental, or should there be only a suspicion that the articles have been seen, no mercy is shown; and it is said that fathers have been the executioners of their own daughters, and husbands of their wives, when such has been the case. I was of course anxious to purchase articles to which such curious customs belong, and spoke to the Tushaúa on the subject. He at length promised to sell them me on my return, stipulating that they were to be embarked at some distance from the village, that there might be no danger of their being seen by the women." (WALLACE, 1853B: 348–349)

These strange, magical instruments – the yuriparí or devils – are made from the stem of a palm and from the bark of a tree in the pea family, *Eperua purpurea*, which is wrapped around the tube in an ever increasing spiral so as to extend in a flaring trumpet shape some distance below the end of the tube. The ceremony, which involves the use of the hallucinogen caapí, was once common among all the Tukanoan peoples of the Rio Vaupés, but even by Wallace's day was becoming less widespread. The deep booming music of the yuriparí represents the voices of the ancestors, and the ceremony is a solemn one of remembrance and initiation, treated with fear and respect by all male members of the group. It is no wonder Wallace found it difficult to persuade the leader of this village to part with one of these magical objects.

In any extended period of fieldwork, there are highs and lows. Wallace was a real optimist, and tended to dwell on the highs – he describes with great gusto the exciting times in seeing native peoples, finding a beautiful bird or butterfly, and in discovering a new palm. But with the highs also came the lows – the insects (the biting kind!), the accidents, and the illnesses. Early on in his travels, near Pará, Wallace accidentally shot himself in the hand as he handled his gun by its muzzle. Part of his hand was blown away, but he apparently did not feel any pain for a few minutes – then wrapped the hand in cotton and bade his host goodbye. He must have recovered rather quickly, as no more is said about this hand injury; the page heading in *Travels on the Amazon* is "A Slight Accident". He was lucky; in the days before antibiotics, such wounds could easily fester and cause death. Other inconveniences of fieldwork are treated similarly, in a rather off-hand and low-key way. Mosquitoes were a constant menace all along the Amazon itself, a torment both night and day, but once on the Rio Negro and in the land of black-water rivers, they were blissfully absent. Other, less familiar, biting insects were also a problem and some made doing even the mundane daily tasks of a naturalist difficult.

"I also suffered a little from another of our insect enemies: the celebrated *chigoe* at length paid us a visit. I found a tender pimple on the side of my foot, which Isidora pronounced to be a "bicho do pé," or chigoe; so preferring to extract it myself, I set to work with a needle, but not being used to the operation, could not get it out entire. I then rubbed a little snuff in the wound, and afterwards felt no more of it. The insect is a minute flea, which burrows into the skin of the toes, where it grows into a large bag of eggs as big as a pea, the insect being just distinguishable as a black speck on one side of it. When it first enters it causes a slight irritation, and if found may then be easily extracted; but when it grows large it is very painful, and if neglected may produce a serious wound." (WALLACE, 1853B: 38–39)

"Senhor L. was here [Jauarité, on the Rio Vaupés] quite a martyr to the chigoes, frequently extracting ten or a dozen a day, which made his feet so full of holes and

Mucura piranha, *Catoprion mento*, Characidae, Lower Rio Negro. One of the herbivorous, or fruit and leaf-eating, piranhas.

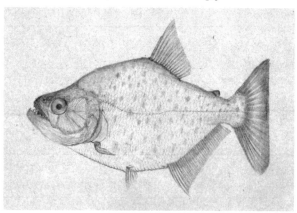

Piranha, *Serrasalmus* species, (*S. rhombeus* group) Characidae (Serrasalminae), Upper Vaupés. The piranhas are much feared for their pack-hunting ferocity. Their ability to bite off chunks of flesh allows them to devour prey much larger than themselves.

wounds as to render walking painful, as I had experienced at Cobáti and Javíta." (WALLACE, 1853B: 303–304)

"Here [São Jeronymo] we were tolerably free of chigoes, but had another plague, far worse, because more continual. We had suffered more or less from piums [simuliid blackflies] in all parts of the river, but here they were in countless myriads, as to render it almost impossible to sit down during the day. ... As it was the torments I suffered when skinning a bird or drawing a fish, can scarcely be imagined by the inexperienced. My feet were so thickly covered with the little blood spots produced by their bites, so as to be of a dark purplish-red colour, and much swelled and inflamed. My hands suffered similarly, but in a less degree, being more constantly in motion. The only means of taking a little rest in the day, was by wrapping up hands and feet in a blanket." (WALLACE, 1853B: 310)

Piums, or simuliid blackflies, are the scourge of the black-water river areas (and also of many white-water regions in the upper Amazon as well). Their larvae develop in fast-flowing, relatively clean water, and they have a terrible bite, leaving a small spot of blood behind. Some people are so sensitive to the bites that they are scarred all over from them, from where they have constantly scratched the unbearable itch. Simuliid blackflies in the Amazon are today more than just annoying. In Africa they are the vectors of the disease river blindness, or onchocerciasis, caused by a filarial parasite introduced by the bite of the fly that eventually makes its human host blind. At some time, which remains a subject of some debate and much discussion, the disease was introduced to the Amazon, and is now spreading through the basin as infected people migrate and come into contact with suitable simuliid blackfly vectors. To Wallace, piums were a terrible nuisance, and mosquitoes were just as, if not more, annoying. We now know that they too are vectors of deadly disease – of yellow fever, which killed his brother, and of malaria, which he certainly contracted while in the Amazon.

But worse even than fever, excruciating insect bites, or raging dysentery was loneliness. Many years spent among strangers can leave one feeling isolated – one

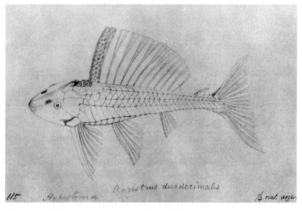

Glyptoperichthys species, Loricariidae. This drawing, in its early stages, illustrates how Wallace went about his work sketching fishes, often in the most trying conditions.

has no companion to talk to, to share experiences with, to commiserate in the low points. When Wallace had resolved to go home to accompany his collections, he thought not only of the green fields and the neat gardens, but of sociable tea tables and of family conversations. High up on the Rio Negro, Wallace made a resolution which would stand him in good stead in his future collecting, although he did not know it at the time.

"Looking after the arrangement of the canoe in the hot sun did not do me much good; and shortly after leaving, I found myself quite knocked up, with headache,

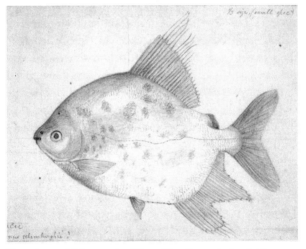

Paco pixuna, *Myleus* species, Characidae (Serrasalminae), Rio Negro. Related to the dreaded piranhas, these fish feed entirely on fruits and leaves and are prized for their sweet flesh.

pains in the back and limbs, and violent fever. I had commenced operations that morning by taking some purgative medicine, and the next day I began taking doses of quinine, drinking plentifully cream of tartar water, though I was so weak and apathetic that at times I could hardly muster resolution to move myself to prepare them. It is at such times that one feels the want of a friend or attendant; for of course it is impossible to get the Indians to do these little things without so much explanation and showing as would require more exertion than doing them oneself. By dint however of another purge, an emetic, washing and bathing, and quinine three times a day, I succeeded in subduing the fever; and in about four days had only a little weakness left, which in a day or two more quite passed away. All this time the Indians went on with the canoe as they liked; for during two days and nights I hardly cared if we sank or swam. While in that apathetic state I was constantly half-thinking, half-dreaming, of all my past life and future hopes, and that they were perhaps all doomed to end here on the Rio Negro.... But with returning health these gloomy thoughts passed away, and I again went on, rejoicing in this my last voyage, and looking forward with firm hope to home, sweet home! I however made an inward vow never to travel again in such wild, unpeopled districts without some civilized companion or attendant." (WALLACE, 1853B: 327–238)

He kept this inward vow. In the Malay Archipelago his constant companion was Ali, a Malay servant and

Iú, *Bactris hirta*.

helper, who served him faithfully through thick and thin for seven years, from 1855 until he left Southeast Asia in 1862. He not only helped Wallace collect, but nursed him when he was sick, and eventually took the surname of Wallace. Never again would Alfred Russel Wallace be left to suffer malaria alone as he had done on the Rio Negro.

Wallace had been an apprentice land surveyor with his elder brother William for seven years, from the age of 14. It was because of this specialised training that he had unique skills which other naturalists of the day lacked. In his scarce spare time during his apprenticeship he would read William's technical books on trigonometry, celestial navigation and elementary astronomy for pleasure, soaking up knowledge along the way. William, like most land surveyors, was something of a geologist although not formally trained. He showed his young brother Alfred fossil oysters and belemnites, and taught him what he knew about the different types of rocks. William also owned an account of the great Trigonometrical Survey of England which detailed how the distances between points were calculated.

"This volume was eagerly read by me, as it gave an account of all the instruments used, including the great theodolite three feet in diameter for measuring the angles of the larger triangles formed by distant mountain tops often twenty or thirty miles apart, and in a few cases more than a hundred miles; the accurate measurement of the base-lines by steel chains laid in wooden troughs, and carefully tightened by exactly the same weight passed over a pulley, while the ends were adjusted by the means of microscopes; the exact temperatures being also taken by several thermometers in order to allow for the contraction or expansion of the chains; ... These wonderfully accurate measurements and calculations impressed me greatly, and with my practical work at surveying and learning the use of that beautiful little instrument the pocket-sextant, opened my mind to the practical applications of mathematics, of which at school I had been taught nothing whatever, ..." (WALLACE, 1905: 109–110)

This early training enabled Wallace to map the unexplored rivers upon which he travelled. His detailed and extremely accurate map of the Rio Negro and the Rio Vaupés, which he produced after his return, brought him to the attention of Sir Roderick Murchison, president of the Royal Geographical Society. Wallace accomplished this detailed map with the bare minimum of instrumentation. "The only instruments I possessed were a prismatic compass, a pocket sextant, and a watch. With the former I took bearings of every point and island visible on my voyage, with sketches, embodying all the information I could obtain from persons, well acquainted with the river, who accompanied me; ..." (WALLACE, 1853C: 217)

Wallace calculated distances in a most novel manner using his watch. He timed canoes both ascending and descending the same stretch of river, then took the mean time to calculate the distance. Of course, different sizes and shapes of canoes travel at slightly different speeds, but by the time Wallace was on the Rio Negro and Rio Vaupés he had had considerable experience with all types of river travel. He also took opportunities to ascertain the rate of travel of various types of canoe in still water, a sort of calibration exercise. On the Rio Negro itself the longitudes of Barra and of San Carlos had been determined accurately by previous travellers, so Wallace filled in the gaps. But what gaps there were! The distance Wallace calculated from the mouth of the Rio Negro to the entrance of the Casiquiare just above San Carlos was 900 miles [about 1450 km]; from the mouth to the supposed source he estimated was 1200 miles [about 1930 km].

In 1561 General Pedro de Ursua attempted the eastward passage of the Amazon from the Spanish colonies of the Andes. In his party was the notorious Lope de Aguirre, who after murdering Ursúa, traversed the Orinoco – but eventually met justice in Trinidad. His name has become a byword for treachery; he is immortalised in the names of nasty rapids all along the eastern Andean slope, and in the extraordinary film entitled *Aguirre, the Wrath of God* (produced and directed by Werner Herzog, released in 1972). Lope de Aguirre, however, did say he had found a sea-level canal connecting the Amazon and Orinoco basins – an assertion others found hard to believe. Two of the great South American explorers verified this fact: Charles-Marie de La Condamine and Alexander von Humboldt. La Condamine was leader of the French Académie de Sciences expedition of the mid-eighteenth century to investigate whether or not the earth bulged at the equator, after which he became the first scientist to descend the Amazon. Humboldt, in the first years of the nineteenth century, went on his famous expedition to the upper Rio Orinoco and Rio Negro from the north, in part to find this disputed connecting channel. This channel, now commonly known as the Casiquiare canal, connects the Rio Negro with the Rio Orinoco near their sources, meaning that the two great rivers of the north bank of the Amazon are really one, with two mouths – one in

Uaracu pinimi, *Leporinus fasciatus*, Anastomidae, Rio Negro.

Uinirama, *Lycengraulis batesii,* Upper Amazon. One of the relatively few species of the anchovy family Engraulidae to occur in freshwater.

Satanoperca daemon, Cichlidae. This fish is a mud "eater" – it sifts through bottom mud to find its food.

the Orinoco delta in eastern Venezuela, and another in the Amazon delta near Pará. This effectively makes most of northeastern South America an island. Water flows from the Orinoco into the Rio Negro, dropping about 25 m. On his way up the Rio Negro, Wallace measured the altitude by measuring the boiling point of water, and was anxious to test the elevation of the Casiquiare, which had been estimated by the great Humboldt.

"Up to São Carlos I had constantly registered the boiling-point of water with an accurate thermometer, made for the purpose, to ascertain the height above the level of the sea. There I had unfortunately broken it, before arriving at this interesting point, the watershed between the Amazon and the Orinoko. I am however inclined to think that the height given by Humboldt for São Carlos is too great. He himself says it is doubtful, as his barometer had got an air-bubble in it, and was emptied and refilled by him, and before returning to the coast was broken, so as to render a comparison of its indications impossible. ... He gives, however, 812 feet as the height of São Carlos above the sea. My observations made a difference of 0.5° of Fahrenheit in the temperature of boiling water between Barra and São Carlos, which would give a height of 250 feet, to which may be added fifty feet for the height of the station at which the observations were made at Barra, making 300 feet. Now the height of Barra above the sea I cannot consider to be more than a hundred feet, for both my own observations and those of Mr. Spruce with the aneroid would make Barra lower than Pará, if the difference of pressure of the atmosphere was solely owing to height, the barometer appearing to stand regularly higher at Barra than at Pará, a circumstance which shows the total inapplicability of that instrument to determine small heights at very great distances. ... Should, as I suspect, the mean pressure of the atmosphere in the interior and on the coasts of South America differ from other causes than elevation, it will be a difficult point ever to accurately ascertain the levels of the interior of this great continent, for the distances are too vast and the forests too impenetrable to allow a line of levels to be carried across it." (WALLACE, 1853B: 245–246)

Wallace was quite right about the difficulty of determining elevation in the Amazon basin. Pará, of course, is at sea level at the mouth of the Amazon, while Barra, more than a thousand kilometres upriver, varies between sea level and just below, depending upon where you stand in the town. Both San Carlos de Rio Negro and the Casiquiare Canal are at about 100 m elevation (approximately 330 feet), or a little bit higher, making Wallace's measurement more or less correct. But if Humboldt was in a slightly different part of the Casiquiare, his measurement could be also more or less correct! The Amazon basin itself is so flat that even Iquitos, in the Peruvian province of Loreto more than two thousand kilometres from the mouth, is only 120 m above sea level. Recent surveys still have large regions of the Amazon basin labelled as "imperfectly known".

However unknown the exact topology of Rio Negro may have been, Wallace truly entered unknown territory on the Rio Vaupés. In the Rio Negro he had joined up with Humboldt's trail, and traders regularly went up and down that great river to Barra and back. The Rio Vaupés however was different. He decided to go up the Rio Vaupés because it was unknown, and there he might find new things. Foremost in his mind however was the area's remoteness and mystery.

"On my return from there [the upper Rio Negro] I shall take a voyage up the great river Uaupés, and another up the Isanna, not so much for my collections, which I do not expect to be very profitable there, but because I am so much interested in the country and the people that I am determined to see and know more of it and them than any other European traveller. If I do not get profit, I hope at least to get some credit as an industrious and persevering traveller." (WALLACE, 1905: 285, LETTER FROM GUIA)

The journey up the Rio Vaupés was incredibly difficult. Wallace and his party of men in canoes passed through an amazing thirty-four rapids or falls (caxoieras) during their ascent towards Juriparí, the last great fall, beyond which – according to the small number of local traders who had ascended the Rio Vaupés further – the river became slow and sluggish again. Portaging canoes around rapids is difficult at the best of times, even with modern equipment and light-weight boats. But for Wallace, with his collecting gear, ever-increasing collections, and provisions for long stays, the whole business was an ordeal – but good for the soul.

"After four days' delay, we at length started, with a comparatively small complement of Indians, but with some extra ones to assist us in passing the several caxoeiras, which occur near at hand. These are the "Piréwa" (Wound), "Uacoroúa" (Goat-sucker), "Maniwára" (White Ant), "Martini" (Fish-trap), "Amána" (Rain), "Tapíra-cúnga" (Tapir's head), "Tapíra eura" (Tapir's mouth), and "Jacaré" (Alligator). Three of these were very bad, the canoe having to be unloaded entirely, and pulled over the dry and uneven rocks. The last was the highest; the river rushing furiously about twenty feet down a rugged slope of rock. The loading and unloading of the canoe three or four times in the course of as many hours, is a great annoyance. Baskets of farinha and salt, of mandiocca cakes and pacovas, are strewn about. Panellas [baskets] are often broken; and when there comes a shower of rain, everything has to be heaped together in a hurry, – palm-leaves cut, and the more perishable articles covered; but boxes, redes, and numerous other articles are sure to be wetted, and very uncomfortable when again placed, with equal hurry and confusion, in the canoe. If I had birds or insects out drying, they were sure to be tumbled, or blown by the wind, or wetted by the rain, and the same fate was shared by my note-books and papers. Articles in

Uiripió, *Copella compta*, Lebiasinidae, source of Rio Negro and Orinoko.

Surubim, *Pseudoplatystoma* species, Pimelodidae, Vaupés, July 1851. These catfish are harvested by the canoe-load and are one of the most important edible fish of the Amazon.

boxes, unless packed tight, were shaken and rumpled by not being carried evenly; so that it was excellent practice of patience, to bear all with philosophical serenity." (WALLACE, 1853C: 350–351)

Wallace never got as far as the last great fall on the Rio Vaupés, the Juriparí – above which the river was reported to widen and become white-water, with plants and animals more like those of the upper Amazon than the Rio Negro. The native peoples living high up on the Rio Vaupés had Spanish coins, knives and ponchos, and reported extensive plains with cattle and men on horseback. All this led Wallace to believe that the Rio Vaupés had its source in the plains of the eastern slopes of the Andes – in which opinion he was more or less right. The Rio Vaupés originates in the Colombian province of Guaviare, on the edge of the llanos – extensive native grasslands that cover much of northeastern Colombia and adjacent Venezuela. The map Wallace made of the Rio Vaupés was not bettered until Hamilton Rice descended the river from Colombia in 1907 to 1908. Rice mapped the source of the Rio Vaupés for the first time, and descended the river from source to mouth, investigating the geology, ethnology and commercial possibilities – particularly of the native, high quality, rubber trees. Further explorations along the Rio Vaupés were not undertaken until the 1940s, when the United States government, worried about the potential shortage of rubber if the Malaysian rubber plantations were to be overrun by the Japanese or Germans during the Second World War, sent Richard Evans Schultes, a Harvard botanist, to investigate the possibilities of rubber tapping in the Colombian Amazon. Almost a hundred years after Wallace's time on the Rio Vaupés, Schultes had similar experiences and adventures among the people of the region, and has published many beautiful books of photographs documenting a lost way of life. (SCHULTES, 1988)

Intent upon the acquisition of information of this previously unexplored region of the Amazon basin, and determined to establish his name as an explorer of note even if he could not get the collections he desired, Wallace tried to estimate his position as accurately as possible, despite his lack of equipment.

"Having only a pocket surveying sextant, without any means of viewing two objects much differing in brilliancy, I endeavoured to obtain the latitude as accurately as I could, first by means of the zenith-distance at noon, obtained by a plumb-line and image of the sun, formed by a lens of about fifteen inches focus; and afterwards, by the meridian altitude of a star, obtained on a calm night, by reflection in a cuya of water. I took much care to ensure an accurate result, and have every reason to believe that the mean of the two observations will not be more than two or three minutes from the truth." (WALLACE, 1853B: 360)

Collectors now carry as a matter of course GPS devices

– sometimes as small as a mobile phone, these global positioning systems rely on the positions of satellites that remain stationary relative to the rotation of the Earth to accurately calculate latitude and longitude – an unheard luxury for Wallace. But technology has its drawbacks too – Wallace was able to look into the night sky high up the Rio Vaupés and see only stars, but today's naturalists, no matter how far from civilisation they are, can always see its traces. By night, winking satellites and the lights of passing far-away jet planes, and by day, white puffy trails from behind these same jets remind us of our own presence on the planet, even deep in the Amazon forests.

Mamyacú, *Asterophysus batrachus*, Auchenipteridae, Upper Rio Negro. This fish was not collected by European scientists until the mid-nineteenth century. If Wallace's collections had not perished with the *Helen*, his specimens would have been among the first.

There are few places in the world today that have not been mapped, and explored, at least from the air. As human beings fill up the planet, none of us will ever again have opportunities and experiences as did Wallace, far from civilisation. Although times for him could be hard and frustrating, they were exhilarating and intellectually stimulating, even in his isolation.

"Being now in a part of the country that no European traveller had ever before visited, I exceedingly regretted my want of instruments to determine the latitude, longitude, and height above the sea. The two last I had no means whatever of ascertaining, having broken my boiling-point thermometer, and lost my smaller one, without being able to replace either. I once thought of scaling up a flask of air, by accurately weighing which on my return, the density of air at that particular time would be obtained, and the height at which a barometer would have stood might be deduced. But, besides that this would only give a single result equal to that of a single barometer observation, there were insuperable difficulties in the way of sealing up the bottle, for whether sealing-wax or pitch were used, or even if the bottle be hermetically sealed, heat must be applied, and at the moment of application would, of course, rarefy the air within the bottle, and so produce in such a delicate operation very erroneous results. My observations however on the heights of the falls we passed, would give their sum as about two hundred and fifty feet; now if we add fifty for the fall of the river between them, we shall obtain three hundred feet, as the probable height of the point I reached above the mouth of the river; and, as I have every reason to believe that that is not five hundred feet above the sea, we shall obtain eight hundred feet as the probable limit of the height of the river at the point I reached, above sea level. Nothing however can accurately determine this fact, but a series of barometer or "boiling-point" observations; and to determine this height above the next great fall, and ascertain the true course and sources of this little-known but interesting and important river, would be an object worth the danger and expense of such a voyage." (WALLACE, 1853B: 359–360)

As Wallace and his men descended the river to return to Barra, they dragged and portaged canoes again and again. As they ascended, so they descended – but more laden with collections. Despite his assertion that the collecting would not really be worth it, and that he was going for the journey itself, Wallace had managed to collect, of course, and he had to protect his precious cargo all the way down the river. The last great rapid they had to descend was the first, and most dangerous, fall on the Rio Vaupés, just before reaching São Jeronymo. The violence of the river here beggared belief.

"There are immense whirlpools which engulf large canoes. The waters roll like ocean waves, and leap up at intervals, forty or fifty feet into the air, as if great subaqueous explosions were taking place." (WALLACE, 1853B: 286)

Barra do Rio Negro (present day Manaus) from the fort, 1851.

"The river had risen considerably since we ascended, and had now reached a higher point than had been known for several years, and the rapids were proportionally more dangerous. I therefore preferred going through the forest, carrying with me two small boxes, containing some insects, and my drawings of fish, the loss of which would be irreparable." (WALLACE, 1853B: 304)

Little did he know what would happen in future – his loss would be irreparable, but those prized fish drawings came through, battered but beautiful.

After deciding to return to England, Wallace went back to Barra, laden with his upper Rio Negro and Rio Vaupés collections. He found to his dismay

Caiauána, *Pimelodus ornatus*, Pimelodidae, Upper Rio Negro.
This predatory catfish is a striking black and white.

Mandú pirocca, *Pimelodella cristata*, Pimelodidae,
Upper Rio Negro.

that the six large crates he had left with a friend to be sent back to England the year before were still sitting in Barra. The customs authorities at the port were afraid they might contain contraband articles and so would not let them be shipped out until Wallace himself came and vouched for their innocence. To add to this inconvenience, he also needed to get a passport to leave the country. To do this he had to inform the local population of his intention to leave Brazil, and get various papers signed by the local authorities. What then followed was a typical bureaucratic tangle.

"As it was necessary to get a passport, I presented myself at the office of the 'Chef de Policia', for the purpose; but was told that I must first advertise my intention of leaving, in the newspaper. I accordingly did so, and about a week after went in again. I was now requested to bring a formal application in writing, to have a passport granted me: I returned, and prepared one, and the next day went in with it; now the Chef was engaged, and he must sign the requisition before anything else could be done. I called again the next day, and now that the requisition was signed, I had a blank form given me to go and get stamped in another office, in a distant part of the city. Off I had to go, – get the stamp, which took two clerks to sign, and paid my eight vintems for it; armed with this, I returned to the police-office, and now, to my surprise, the passport was actually made out and given to me; and on paying another twelve vintems (sixpence), I was at

Bussu, *Manicaria saccifera*. "The 'bussu' produces the largest entire leaves of any known palm and for this reason, as well as on account of their firm and rigid texture, they form the very best and durable thatch…A well-made thatch of 'bussu' will last ten or twelve years, and an Indian will often take a week's voyage in order to get a canoe-load of leaves to cover his house."

liberty to leave Barra whenever I could; for as to leaving it whenever I pleased, that was out of the question." (WALLACE, 1853B: 374–375)

Today's collectors are apparently more regulated than was Wallace. Permission must now be obtained from the authorities in the country concerned to collect and export specimens – both the Convention on International Trade in Endangered Species (CITES) and the Convention on Biological Diversity (CBD) help to prevent exploitation and over-collecting of increasingly endangered plants and animals. But although paperwork is dull and tedious for a field biologist, the regulation system has its positive side. In most places today collectors are required to have a local counterpart – a scientist or student of the country concerned. This is a wonderful system; it helps to facilitate the bureaucracy inherent in regulation, but more importantly it serves to bring scientists of different cultures and backgrounds together, making for the true sharing of experience – something that immeasurably benefits both parties. Wallace went where he wanted, and had to deal with minimal paperwork (but did not escape it entirely!), but he missed the intellectual company of local scientists that most modern collectors enjoy.

Wallace had to wait for transport down the Amazon to Pará – some 1200 kilometres. He was not alone in wanting transport. No vessel had arrived from Pará for months and the city of Barra was in a state of desperation. Food supplies had long since run short, and people were reduced to eating the bare minimum. A vessel had been due to arrive, but it sank just as it was rounding a bend in the river near Barra. The journey up river at that time of year took from seventy days to three months, as the canoes had to be pulled against the current of the mighty Amazon. Several vessels were leaving, but had no room for Wallace and his collections – from which he did not want to be parted. A friend of Wallace's, however, was sending a small canoe to Pará once it returned from a journey on the Solimões, and on this he was guaranteed passage. So he just had to wait for it to arrive.

Once the canoe did arrive, he had to extract his six cases from the customs house – this was easily accomplished by paying a small amount of duty – and gather up his remaining collections and other things. By this time he also carried with him quite a few live animals, his "menagerie", which he intended to take home with him. He had been caring for these animals all the way down the Rio Negro and through the long wait in Barra, and was quite attached to them. Unfortunately for Wallace, but fortunately for the bird, his prize toucan escaped at the last minute before the canoe left Barra.

"Of the hundred live animals which I had purchased or had had given to me, there now only remained thirty-four, consisting of five monkeys, two macaws, twenty parrots and paroquets of twelve different species, five small birds, a white-crested Brazilian pheasant, and a toucan." (WALLACE, 1853B: 382–383)

The journey from Barra to Pará took from the 10th of June until the 2nd of July – twenty-two days in a small canoe (really more like a boat, as Wallace had a small cabin in which to sleep), surviving a violent storm at night, missing his friend Bates at Santarém, making last minute sketches of palms needed to complete the collection, and all the while suffering from "fits of ague" (WALLACE, 1853B: 389) – the recurrent fevers of malaria. Arriving in Pará, Wallace thought he was fortunate in finding that a vessel in port would probably sail for London within the week. He obtained passage, and in the remaining days before departing tried to go out into

Mandobé, *Ageneiosus brevifilis*, Auchenipteridae, Upper Rio Negro. An important food fish along the Rio Negro.

the forest, but found himself too weak from the shivering and sickness any exertion brought on to continue. So he rested and remained as quiet as possible until the ship departed. Yellow fever was still a problem in Pará, and Wallace did not want to be cut off just as he was about to profit from all his hard work of the last four years!

The brig *Helen*, weighing 235 tons and belonging to Captain John Turner, left the port of Pará on the 12th of July 1852, bound for London. On board were Wallace, still ill and feverish, his menagerie, and all his collections from four years of intensive collecting in the most unexplored parts of the Rio Negro and Rio Vaupés – a precious cargo indeed. The bulk of the cargo, and the real commercial reason for the *Helen*'s voyage to England, consisted of "about a hundred and twenty tons of India-rubber, and a quantity of cocoa, annatto, piassaba, and balsam of capivi." (WALLACE, 1853B: 391) Balsam of capivi is the sap of the tree *Copaifera officinalis* in the pea family, which was and still is used in the manufacture of varnishes and lacquers, as well as medicinally. The substance is oily, resinous and extremely volatile and was usually stored in casks and stowed packed all around by wet sand. The load of balsam of capivi aboard the *Helen* however, was not all packed correctly. Twenty casks were packed in dry rice chaff rather than sand; a disastrous mistake as it turned out. For about three weeks everything went well, the winds were light and the weather fine. But on the 6th of August 1852, at latitude 30°30' north and longitude 52° west, in the middle of the Atlantic Ocean far from land, the situation changed for the worse.

"On that morning after breakfast, I was reading in the cabin, when the Captain came down and said to me, 'I'm afraid the ship's on fire; come and see what you think of it,' and proceeded to examine the lazaretto, or small hole under the floor where the provisions are kept, but no signs of fire were visible there. We then went on deck to the fore part of the ship, where we found a dense vapoury smoke issuing from the forecastle. The fore hatchway was immediately opened, and, the smoke issuing there also, the men were set to work clearing out part of the cargo. After throwing out some quantity without any symptom of approaching the seat of the fire, we opened the after hatchway; and here smoke was much more dense, and in a very short time became so suffocating, that the men could not stay in the hold to throw out more cargo, so they were set to work pouring in water, while others proceeded to the cabin, and now found abundance of smoke issuing from the lazaretto, whence it had entered through the joints of the bulkhead which separated it from the hold. Attempts were now made to break this bulkhead down; but the planks were so thick and the smoke so unbearable that it could not be effected, as no man could remain in the lazaretto to make more than a couple of blows. The

Canderu, *Cetopsis coecutiens*, Cetopsidae, Upper Rio Negro. Like the piranhas, these fish hunt in packs and bite chunks of flesh from their prey. Many early accounts of piranha attacks may be attributable to these catfish.

Acestrorhynchus falcirostris, Acestrorhynchidae, Vaupés. A fearsome predator, this species has razor-sharp teeth.

cabin table was therefore removed, and a hole attempted to be cut in the cabin floor, so as to be able to pour water immediately on the seat of the fire, which appeared to be where the balsam was stowed. ... Seeing that there was now little chance of our being able to extinguish the fire, the Captain thought it prudent to secure our own safety, and called all hands to get out the boats, and such necessaries as we should want, in case of being obliged to take to them. ... All now were in great activity. Many little necessaries had to be hunted up from their hiding places. The cook was sent for corks, to plug the holes in the bottoms of the boats. Now no one knew where a rudder had been put away; now the thowl-pins were missing. The oars had to be searched for, and spars to serve as masts. ... The Captain was looking after his chronometer, sextant, barometer, charts, compasses, and books of navigation; the seamen were getting their clothes into huge canvas bags; all were lugging about pilot-coats, blankets, south-westers, and oilskin coats and trowsers; and I went down into the cabin, now suffocatingly hot and full of smoke, to see what was worth saving. I got my watch and a small tin box containing some shirts and a couple of old note-books, with some drawings of plants and animals, and scrambled with them up on deck. Many clothes and a large portfolio of drawings and sketches remained in my berth; but I did not care to venture down again, in fact felt a kind of apathy about saving anything, that I can hardly now account for." (WALLACE, 1853B: 391–394)

The lifeboats were made ready, leaking as they were, loaded with the "necessaries", and the crew, with Wallace, continued to attempt to stem the blaze, which by this time was completely out of control.

"Now, too, we could hear in the hold the balsam bubbling, like some great boiling cauldron, which told of such intense heat, that we knew the flames must soon break out. And so it was, for in less than half an hour the fire burst through the cabin-floor into the berths, and consuming rapidly through the dry pine-wood, soon flamed up through the skylight. There was now a scorching heat on the quarter deck, and we saw that all hope was over, and that we must in a few minutes be driven by the terrible element to take refuge on the scarcely less dangerous one, which heaved and swelled its mighty billows a thousand miles on every side of us." (WALLACE, 1853B: 394)

All hands were now ordered into the lifeboats, and Wallace, while sliding down the rope into the boat, was so weak he could not hold on properly and rubbed all the skin off his hands. The boats themselves were so leaky that all the men were obliged to bale furiously, including Wallace. This must have been terribly painful with fresh wounds on the palms of his hands, but in his typically modest way he describes it as merely "a most intense smarting and burning on my scarified fingers." (WALLACE, 1853B: 394) They stayed close to the burning ship to watch the fire's progress and to take advantage of

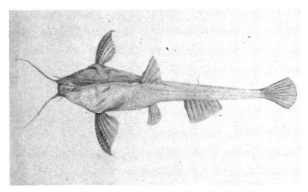

Bunocephalus coracoideus or *B. aleuropsis*, Aspredinidae, Upper Vaupés. This is the extremely well-camouflaged banjo catfish of the aquarium trade.

the light of the flames at night which might attract any passing ships to their rescue. Wallace felt for the animals he had had on board, but, like his collections they were more or less left to their fate.

"Many of the parrots, monkeys and other animals we had on board, were already burnt or suffocated; but several had retreated to the bowsprit out of reach of the flames, appearing to wonder what was going on, and quite unconscious of the fate that awaited them. We tried to get some of them into the boats, but going as near as we could venture; but they did not seem to be at all aware of the danger they were in, and would not make any attempt to reach us. As the flames caught the base of the bowsprit, some of them ran back and jumped into the midst of the fire. Only one parrot escaped: he was sitting on a rope hanging from the bowsprit, and this burning above him let him fall into the water, where after floating a little way, we picked him up." (WALLACE, 1853B: 395)

They floated all night alongside the burning wreckage, a very dangerous operation, as the many burnt pieces of wreckage could easily have stove in the fragile and leaking lifeboats. Their mooring ropes had burnt, so they kept the ship in sight by rowing towards it – in a strong swell, and at night this must have been a tricky manoeuvre.

"We were incessantly baling the whole night. Ourselves and everything in the boats were thoroughly drenched, so we got little repose: if for an instant we dozed off into forgetfulness, we soon woke up again to the realities of our position, and to see the red glare which our burning vessel cast over us. It was now a magnificent spectacle, for the decks had completely burnt away, and as it heaved and rolled with the swell of the sea, presented its interior towards us filled with liquid flame – a fiery furnace tossing restlessly upon the ocean." (WALLACE, 1853B: 396)

"I cannot attempt to describe my feelings and thoughts during these events. I was surprised to find myself very cool and collected. I hardly thought it possible we should escape, and remember thinking it almost foolish to save my watch and the little money I had at hand. However, after being in the boats some days I began to have more hope, and regretted not having saved some new shoes, cloth coat and trousers, hat, etc., which I might have done with a little more trouble. My collections, however, were in the hold, and were irretrievably lost. And now I began to think that almost all the reward of my four years of privation and danger was lost. What I had hitherto sent home had little more than paid my expenses, and what I had with me in the *Helen* I estimated would have realized about £500. But even all this might have gone with little regret had not by far the richest part of my own private collection gone also." (WALLACE, 1905:305,

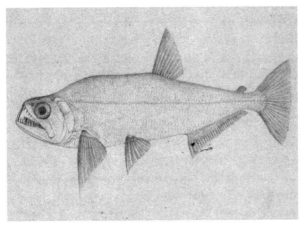

Pirantera or wisimati, *Hydrolycus tatauia*, Characidae, Javita, sources of Orinoco. This drawing was one of Wallace's favourites, and was reproduced in his autobiography.

FROM A LETTER TO RICHARD SPRUCE FROM ABOARD THE *JORDESON*, DATED SUNDAY 19 SEPTEMBER 1852)

They tried to steer the boats in the direction of Bermuda, but were frustrated by the squally winds and heavy rains. The sails became saturated with salt, and the men were even unable to catch the rain to use as drinking water. As they went however the boats leaked less and less, as the wood swelled, which was a small blessing. All the men became sunburnt and blistered, having no shelter from the blazing sun, and as the days dragged on, they had to ration their little remaining water – leaving them all parched with thirst. Wallace, however, continued to observe with a true naturalist's eye.

"At night two boobies, large dusky sea-birds with very long wings, flew about us. During the night I saw several meteors, and in fact could not be in a better position for observing them, than lying on my back in a small boat in the middle of the Atlantic." (WALLACE, 1853B: 397–398)

They were in the lifeboats for nine days, until on the evening of the 15th of August, when nearly in despair of seeing a ship or making it all the way to Bermuda, they spotted a ship tacking towards them – apparently having seen their sail. They were saved! The men rowed joyfully and heartily towards the vessel, and they were received "kindly on board" (WALLACE, 1853B: 400) the *Jordeson*, belonging to Captain Venables, who was coming from Cuba with a load of tropical hardwoods for eventual sale in England. They were lucky – the *Jordeson* picked them up at latitude 32°48' north, longitude 60°27' west, still some two hundred miles short of Bermuda. It was also the hurricane season, and their chances of reaching Bermuda at the rate they were going were slim indeed. Wallace was full of emotion, and began to think about his situation and position.

"That night I could not sleep. Home and all its pleasures seemed now within my grasp; and crowding thoughts, and hopes and fears, made me pass a more restless night than I should have done, had we still been in the boats, with diminished hopes of rescue." (WALLACE, 1853B: 400)

"It was now, when the danger appeared past, that I began to feel fully the greatness of my loss. With what pleasure I had looked upon every rare and curious insect I had added to my collection! How many times, when almost overcome with the ague, had I crawled into the forest and been rewarded by some unknown and beautiful species! How many places, which no European foot but my own had trodden, would have been recalled to my memory by the rare birds and insects they had furnished to my collection! How many weary days and weeks had I passed, upheld only by the fond hope of bringing home many new and beautiful forms from those wild regions; every one of which would be endeared to me by the recollections they would call up, which should prove that I had not wasted the advantages I had enjoyed, and would give me occupation and amusement for many years to come! And now everything was gone, and I had not one specimen to illustrate the unknown lands I had trod, or to call back the recollection of the wild scenes I had beheld! But such regrets I knew were vain, and I tried to think as little as possible about what might have been, and to occupy myself with the state of things which actually existed." (WALLACE, 1853B: 400–401)

Conditions on the *Jordeson* were, if anything, worse than those on the lifeboats. Their arrival had exactly doubled the complement of men on board, and rations were short before they were picked up! Wallace longed for the dried fish he had tired of along the Amazon – the "fiel amigo", dried, salted pirarucú, which with farinha was always on hand even when other food failed. The ship itself was rotting – the men in their hammocks in the forecastle apparently pulled great handfuls of rotten wood out from where it was constantly wet, and in the waves, water sprayed in everywhere. The ship itself rolled along at only five knots maximum speed, so the journey took them a month and a half, a long time in a rotten ship in the Atlantic. The voyage was also not without incident and excitement for the ever-observant and intellectually energetic Wallace.

"Having never seen a great gale or storm at sea, I had some desire to witness the phenomenon, and now have been completely gratified. The first we had about a fortnight ago. In the morning there was a strong breeze and the barometer had fallen nearly a half inch during the night and continued sinking, so the captain commenced taking in sail, and while getting the royals and studding-sails, the wind increased so as to split the mainsail, fore-topsail, fore-trysail, and jib, and it was some hours before they could be got off her, and the main-topsail and fore-sail double reefed. We then went flying along, the whole ocean a mass of boiling foam, the crests of the waves being carried in spray over our decks. The sea did not get up immediately, but by night it was very rough, the ship plunging and rolling most fearfully, the sea pouring in a deluge over the top of her bulwarks, and sometimes up over the cabin skylight. ... Three days ago we had another gale, more severe than the former one – a regular equinoctial, which lasted two entire days and nights, and split one of the newest and strongest sails on the ship. The rolling and plunging were fearful, the bowsprit going completely under the water, and the ship being heavily laden with mahogany, fustic, and other heavy woods from Cuba, strained and creaked tremendously, and leaked to the extent that the pumps were obliged to be kept constantly going, and the continued click-clack, click-clack all through the night was a most disagreeable and nervous sound." (WALLACE, 1905: 308, LETTER TO RICHARD SPRUCE FROM ABOARD THE *JORDESON*)

They landed at Deal on the 1st of October 1852, narrowly escaping a violent storm in which many ships were lost in the English Channel, "thankful for having escaped so many dangers, and glad to tread once more on English ground." (WALLACE, 1853B: 403)

Arriving in England with only the clothes on his back and his small tin box rescued from the fire, Wallace was taken in hand by Samuel Stevens, his agent. Stevens took Wallace to a tailor to get him a new woollen suit, arranged for him lodgings with Stevens' own mother, and generally helped him to integrate back into English society – always a difficult task after an extended

Canderú mirí, Upper Rio Negro. This parasitic catfish is a species of the genus *Pseudovandellia* in the family Trichomycteridae. "The stomach is generally more or less filled with blood as it [the fish] attaches itself to other fish and aquatic animals and sucks them. This minute fish enters the urinary passage of men and woman, wounds, and extracts blood within, and all efforts to extract it are usually unavailing."

period of fieldwork, never mind one that included such an adventure and narrow escape as Wallace had just survived! His friends all commiserated with his loss – Bates, writing to Stevens, expressed it better than many scientists, and even Brazilian friends wrote to sympathise.

"I am really sorry for Wallace's loss. Had it been my case I think I should have gone desperate, because, so far as regards the unique specimens, the journal &c., such a loss is irreparable." (BATES, 1853: 4114)

"... I was much grieved at the misfortunes that befell our good friend Alfredo! My dear Senhor Spruce, what labours he performed for mankind, and what trouble to lose all his work for four years; but yet his life is saved, and that is the most precious for a man. Do me the favour, when you write to Senhor Alfredo, to give him my kind remembrances. The mother of my children also begs you to give her remembrances to Senhor Alfredo, also tell him from me that if he ever comes to these parts again he will find that I shall be to him the same Lima as before, and give him more remembrances from the bottom of my heart ..." (WALLACE, 1905: 312, LETTER FROM JOÃO ANTONIO DE LIMA TO RICHARD SPRUCE, DATED SAN JOAQUIM, 7 JUNE 1853, TRANSLATED FROM THE PORTUGUESE BY WALLACE)

But Wallace was not desperate; he was not like that. Even aboard ship he thought not of what might have been, but what was, and this is what characterised him and was part of what made him such a great collector and naturalist. If one is occupied with thoughts of possibilities, observations of things happening are missed – something that rarely happened to Wallace! Only four days after his return, Wallace was already thinking of the future, and planning his next move.

"How I begin to envy you in that glorious country where 'the sun shines forever unchangeably bright,' where farinha abounds, and of bananas and plantains there is no lack! Fifty times since I left Pará have I vowed, if I reached England, never to trust myself more on the ocean. But good resolutions soon fade, and I am already only doubtful whether the Andes or the Philippines are to be the scene of my next wanderings. However, for the next six months I am a fixture here in London, as I am determined to make up for lost time by enjoying myself as much as possible for awhile. I am fortunate in having about £200 insured by Mr. Stevens' foresight, so I must be contented, though it is hard to have nothing to show of what I took such pains to procure." (WALLACE, 1905: 309, LETTER TO RICHARD SPRUCE)

Wallace was indeed fortunate in Stevens' foresight, without it he would have been penniless. Stevens had also seen to it that Wallace's name was recognised in London biological circles, by reading at the Zoological Society several papers sent by Wallace from the Amazon – one on the umbrella bird and another on the fishes allied to *Gymnotus*, the electric eel. Because his reputation preceded him, he could attend meetings of the Zoological and Entomological Societies, where he met the leaders of London scientific society.

"It was at this time I first saw Huxley. ... I was particularly struck with his wonderful power of making a difficult and rather complex subject perfectly intelligible and extremely interesting to persons, who like myself, were absolutely ignorant of the whole group. ... From that time I always looked up to Huxley as being immeasurably superior to myself in scientific knowledge, and supposed him to be much older than I was. Many years afterwards I was surprised to find that he was really younger." (WALLACE, 1905: 323–324)

Later, Thomas Henry Huxley and Alfred Russel Wallace would be forever linked by the theory of evolution by natural selection and Darwin's *On the Origin of Species*, but to the young, returned naturalist the London luminaries were extremely impressive. Wallace himself made his own impact; he read a paper on Amazonian monkeys to the Zoological Society

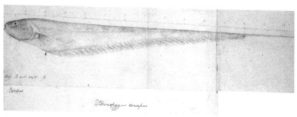

Sarrapu, Tomo. This is one of the so-called 'electric eels', which uses electric fields to navigate in the murky waters of the Amazon.

and greatly impressed the president of the Royal Geographical Society, the reputedly crusty and hard-to-please Sir Roderick Murchison, with his map of the Rio Negro and the Rio Vaupés, both previously unexplored. This map, and his two Amazonian books, both published in 1853, were the fruits of his memory and of the contents of the small tin box he took from the *Helen*. All that had survived from the Amazon adventure were his notes for the Rio Negro map, his pencil sketches of palms and fishes, and a few tiny notebooks – but even more important than those things, Wallace's sense of adventure and his overwhelming intellect had survived, still seeking knowledge about the "origin of species".

Criticisms of his books were many. Darwin deplored the lack of facts in Wallace's travel book, *Narrative of Travels on the Amazon and Rio Negro*. That does seem terribly unfair, considering that all English scientific society, including Darwin, knew his collections had all

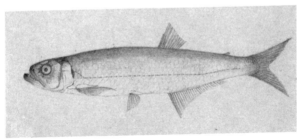

Apapaí, *Agonaites halecinus*, Characidae, Rio Negro (St. Isabel, net).

been lost. The same applies to the little book on palms
– but interestingly, the pencil sketches are much more
accurate than the lithographs that Fitch, the premier
botanical illustrator of his day, made from them.
One wonders if he did a slap-dash job for the young
unknown naturalist? If he did, Wallace was probably too
polite to fuss.

Despite the critics and the crushing loss of his precious
collections he continued to plot out the future as a
naturalist. By the end of 1853, Wallace had decided on
his next move, which was characteristically bold.

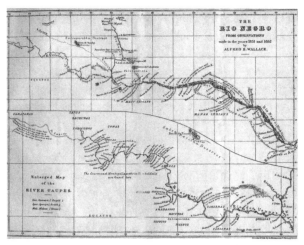

Wallace's map of the Rio Negro and the Rio Vaupés. The original
large-scale map is held in the archives of the Royal Geographical
Society, London.

"During my constant attendance at the meetings of the Zoological and Entomological Societies, and visits to the insect and bird departments of the British Museum, I had obtained sufficient information to satisfy me that the very finest field for an exploring and collecting naturalist was to be found in the great Malayan Archipelago, of which just sufficient was known to prove its wonderful richness, while no part of it, with the one exception of the island of Java, had been well explored as regards its natural history. Sir James Brooke had recently become Rajah of Sarawak, while the numerous Dutch settlements in Celebes and the Moluccas offered great facilities for a traveller. So far as known also, the country was generally healthy, and I determined that it would be much better for me to go to such a new country than to return to the Amazon, where Bates had already been successfully collecting for five years, and where I knew there was a good bird-collector who had long been at work in the upper part of the river towards the Andes.

As the journey to the East was an expensive one, I was advised to try to get a free passage in some Government ship. Through my paper on the Rio Negro, I had made the acquaintance of Sir Roderick Murchison, then President of the Royal Geographical Society, and one of the most accessible and kindly men of science. On calling upon him and stating my wishes, he at once agreed to make an application on my behalf for a passage to some Malayan port, and as he was personally known to many members of the Government and had great influence with them, a passage was promised me on the first ship going to those seas." (WALLACE, 1905: 326–327)

Passage on a government ship did not work out, as it was re-routed to the Crimea with war supplies, but in March of 1854, again through the offices of Murchison, Wallace was heading to the East – aboard a commercial steamer on a first-class ticket. He was to assure his place in history by his work in the Malay Archipelago, and by his bombshell of an essay entitled '*On the Tendency of Varieties to Depart Indefinitely from the Original Type*', written after a malarial fever on the island of Ternate and sent in a letter to Charles Darwin in 1858. This framework theory of how species evolve, the fruit of many years of thinking about the "problem of [the] origin of species" pushed Darwin into publishing his magnum opus *On the Origin of Species*. The rest is history. But none of that would have been possible had Wallace not been nature's apprentice in the Amazon and survived – with his intellect and great courage undimmed – ordeals that would have broken a lesser man.

Reading

Selected books and articles, and material quoted in
the text.

Balick, Michael J. 1980. Wallace, Spruce and Palm Trees
of the Amazon: an Historical Perspective. *Botanical
Museum Leaflets* 28 (3): 263–269.

Bates, Henry Walter. 1853. Proceedings of Natural
History Collectors in Foreign Countries, letter to Mr.
S. Stevens dated March 10, 1853, from Santarem. *The
Zoologist* 11: 4113–4117.

Bates, Henry Walter. 1863. *The Naturalist on the River
Amazons, a Record of Adventures, Habits of Animals,
Sketches of Brazilian and Indian Life, and Aspects of
Nature Under the Equator, During Eleven Years of Travel.*
2 volumes. John Murray, London.

Beddall, Barbara G. (ed.) 1969. *Wallace and Bates in the Tropics: An Introduction to the Theory of Natural Selection.* Collier-MacMillan Ltd., London.

Brackman, Arnold C. 1980. *A Delicate Arrangement: The Strange Case of Charles Darwin and Alfred Russel Wallace.* Times Books, New York.

Brooks, John L. 1984. *Just Before the Origin: Alfred Russel Wallace's Theory of Evolution.* Colombia University Press, New York.

Camerini, Jane R. 1993. Evolution, Biogeography and Maps: An Early History of Wallace's Line. *Isis* 84: 700–727.

Camerini, Jane R. 1996. Wallace in the Field. *Osiris*, second series, 11: 44–65.

Chambers, Robert [published anonymously]. 1844. *Vestiges of the Natural History of Creation.* John Churchill, London [the book went through many editions as an anonymous publication until the author's identity was revealed in 1882].

Clements, Harry. 1983. *Alfred Russel Wallace: Biologist and Social Reformer.* Hutchison & Co., London.

Darwin, C. 1839. *Journal of Researches into the Geology and Natural History of the Various Countries Visited by H.M.S. Beagle.* Henry Colburn, London [Wallace may have read the widely distributed 1845 second edition].

Davis, E. Wade. 1996. *One River: Explorations and Discoveries in the Amazon Rainforest.* Simon & Schuster, New York.

Edwards, William H. 1847. *A Voyage Up the River Amazon, Including a Residence at Pará*. John Murray, London.

Fichman, Martin. 1981. *Alfred Russel Wallace*. Twayne Publishers, Boston.

George, Wilma. 1964. *Biologist Philospher; A Study of the Life and Writings of Alfred Russel Wallace*. Abelard-Schumann, London.

George, Wilma. 1979. Alfred Wallace, the gentle trader: collecting in Amazonia and the Malay Archipelago 1848–1862. *Journal of the Society for the Bibliography of Natural History* 9 (4): 503–514.

Govaerts, Rafael and John Dransfield. 2005. *World Checklist of Palms*. Kew Publishing, Kew.

Hooker, William J. 1854. Notices of Books – review of Wallace's Palm Trees of the Amazon. *Hooker's Journal of Botany* 6: 61–62.

Humboldt, Alexander von. 1818. *Personal Narrative on Travels to the Equinoctial Regions of the New Continent During the Years 1799 to 1804*. [originally published as *Voyage aux régions équinoxiales du nouveau continent…*]. English translation by H. M. Williams, 5 volumes. Longman, Hurst, Rees, Orme & Browne, London [an abridged version of the *Personal Narrrative*, translated by J. Williams, was published by Penguin Books in 1995].

Knapp, Sandra, Lynn Sanders and William Baker. 2002. Alfred Russel Wallace and the palms of the Amazon. *Palms* 46: 109–119.

McKinney, H. Lewis. 1972. *Wallace and Natural Selection*. Yale University Press, New Haven.

Nelson, Gareth. 1995. When I Was Alive by Alfred Russel Wallace. *The Linnean* 11(2): 20–31.

Oosterzee, Penny van. 1997. *Where Worlds Collide: The Wallace Line*. Cornell University Press, Ithaca and London.

Prance, Ghillean T. 1999. Alfred Russel Wallace (presidential address at the unveiling of the portrait of ARW at Linnean Society in 1998). *The Linnean* 15(1): 18–36.

Quammen, David. 1996. *The Song of the Dodo: Island Biogeography in an Age of Extinction*. Hutchinson, London.

Raby, Peter. 1996. *Bright Paradise: Victorian Scientific Travellers*. Chatto & Windus, London.

Schultes, Richard E. 1988. *Where the Gods Reign: Plants and Peoples of the Colombian Amazon*. Synergetic Press, London & Oracle, Arizona.

Smith, Charles H. (ed.) 1991. *Alfred Russel Wallace: An Anthology of his Shorter Writings*. Oxford University Press, Oxford.

Spruce, Richard. 1855. *MS letter to Sir William Hooker*, dated 1855 [held in the archives of the Royal Botanic Gardens, Kew].

Wallace, Alfred Russel. 1848. *MS letter to Sir William Hooker*, dated Pará August 20th 1848 [held in the archives of the Royal Botanic Gardens, Kew].

Wallace, Alfred Russel. 1849. Journey to Explore the Province of Pará [extract from a letter dated 23 October 1848 from Wallace and Bates to Stevens]. *Annals and Magazine of Natural History* 3, series 2: 74–75.

Wallace, Alfred Russel. 1850A. Journey to Explore the Natural History of South America [extract of letter dated 12 September 1849 from Wallace to Stevens]. *Annals and Magazine of Natural History* 5, series 2:156–157.

Wallace, Alfred Russel. 1850B. Journey to Explore the Natural History of the Amazon River [extracts of letters dated 15 November 1849 and 20 March 1850 from Wallace to Stevens]. *Annals and Magazine of Natural History* 6, series 2: 494–496.

Wallace, Alfred Russel. 1850C. On the Umbrella Bird (*Cephalopterus ornatus*) "Ueramimbé". *Proceedings of the Zoological Society of London* 18: 206–207 [from a letter dated 10 March 1850, read by Stevens at the meeting of 23 July 1850].

Wallace, Alfred Russel. 1852A. Letter concerning loss of collections, dated 19 October 1852. *The Zoologist* 10: 3641–3642.

Wallace, Alfred Russel. 1852B. On the Monkeys of the Amazon. *Proceedings of the Zoological Society of London* 20:107–110 [read at meeting of 14 December 1852].

Wallace, Alfred Russel. 1853A. *Palm Trees of the Amazon and Their Uses*. Van Voorst, London.

Wallace, Alfred Russel. 1853B. *A Narrative of Travels*

on the Amazon and Rio Negro, with an Account of the Native Tribes and Observations on the Climate, Geology, and Natural History of the Amazon Valley. Reeve & Co., London.

Wallace, Alfred Russel. 1853C. On the Rio Negro. *Journal of the Royal Geographical Society* 23: 212–217 [read at meeting of 13 June 1853].

Wallace, Alfred Russel. 1853D. On Some Fishes Allied to *Gymnotus. Proceedings of the Zoological Society of London* 21: 75–76 [read at meeting of 12 July 1853].

Wallace, Alfred Russel. 1854A. On the Insects Used for Food by the Indians of the Amazon. *Transactions of the Entomological Society of London* 2, new series part 8: 241–244 [read at meeting 6 June 1853].

Wallace, Alfred Russel. 1854B. On the Habits of the Butterflies of the Amazon Valley. *Transactions of the Entomological Society of London* 2, new series part 8: 253–264 [read at meeting 7 November and 5 December 1853].

Wallace, Alfred Russel. 1905. *My Life: A Record of Events and Opinions.* Volumes 1 and 2. Chapman & Hall, Ltd., London [all quotes are from volume 1].

Wallace, Alfred Russel (edited, translated and organised by Mônica de Toledo-Pizo Ragazzo). 2002. *Peixes do Rio Negro/Fishes of the Rio Negro*. Imprenta Oficial do Estado, Saõ Paulo, Brazil.

Williams-Ellis, Amabel. 1966. *Darwin's Moon: A Biography of Alfred Russel Wallace*. Blackie, London & Glasgow.

Index

PICTURE CREDITS   PAGES 29,
33, 39, 40, 47, 52, 54, 57, 59-60,
62, 68, 82, 86, 90, 97, 99, 104-
106, 108, 110, 119-120, 122,
131, 147, 150 © THE LINNEAN
SOCIETY OF LONDON. ALL
OTHER IMAGES © NATURAL
HISTORY MUSEUM, LONDON.

FIRST PUBLISHED BY THE
NATURAL HISTORY MUSEUM,
CROMWELL ROAD, LONDON SW7
5BD. THIS EDITION PUBLISHED
2013
© NATURAL HISTORY MUSEUM,
LONDON, 1999, 2013

ISBN 978 0 565 09330 3

A CATALOGUE RECORD FOR
THIS BOOK IS AVAILABLE
FROM THE BRITISH LIBRARY.

PRINTED BY TJ INTERNATIONAL
LTD.

MIX
Paper from
responsible sources
FSC® C013056
www.fsc.org